UNDERSTANDING
SCRIPTURE

ivp

UNDERSTANDING SCRIPTURE

AN OVERVIEW OF THE BIBLE'S ORIGIN, RELIABILITY AND MEANING

EDITED BY WAYNE GRUDEM,
C. JOHN COLLINS AND
THOMAS R. SCHREINER

INTER-VARSITY PRESS
Norton Street, Nottingham NG7 3HR, England
Email: ivp@ivpbooks.com
Website: www.ivpbooks.com

First published 2012

British Library Cataloguing in Publication Data
A catalogue record for this book is available from the British Library.

ISBN: 978-1-84474-564-7

Typeset in the United States of America
Printed and bound in Great Britain by Ashford Colour Press Ltd, Gosport,
Hampshire

*Inter-Varsity Press publishes Christian books that are true to the Bible and that
communicate the gospel, develop discipleship and strengthen the church for its
mission in the world.*

*Inter-Varsity Press is closely linked with the Universities and Colleges Christian
Fellowship, a student movement connecting Christian Unions in universities and
colleges throughout Great Britain, and a member movement of the International
Fellowship of Evangelical Students. Website: www.uccf.org.uk*

CONTENTS

CONTENTS

Part 1

INTERPRETING
THE BIBLE

1

INTERPRETING THE BIBLE: AN INTRODUCTION

Daniel Doriani

The Bible contains sixty-six books, written in three languages over fifteen hundred years by dozens of authors writing in numerous genres for diverse audiences. Scripture is clear enough that anyone can grasp the essentials of the faith. At the same time, extensive reading leads to riddles: Why does Moses apparently condone polygamy and slavery? What is a denarius? Who is Apollyon? Why do the apostles care about meat that is offered to idols?

THE REQUIREMENTS FOR INTERPRETATION

Skill in interpretation is needed to gain the most from the Bible. When Scriptures are read in the church, leaders can answer questions and orient listeners to its great themes. Still, people rightly desire to read and understand the Bible for themselves (Jer. 31:31–34; 1 John 2:27).

Interpretation of the Bible requires technical skill and spiritual receptivity. Though all God's people have a significant ability to read and understand the great teachings of the Bible in their own language (see Deut. 6:6–7; Pss. 1:1–2; 19:7; 119:130; 1 Cor. 1:2; Eph. 3:4; Col. 4:16), there also remain more detailed and precise questions about meaning that sometimes require technical knowledge of Greek and Hebrew, as well as of Scripture's historical, cultural, and intellectual backgrounds. Here interpretation resembles the reading of dense poetry or constitutional documents. Interpretation is also an art, mastered not by rigid adherence to procedures but by long practice conducted under tutors. Interpretation is also a spiritual task. To read the Bible is not to dissect a lifeless text that only contains marks on a page. As people read Scripture, Scripture reads them, questions them, reveals their thoughts (Heb. 4:12)—and it leads to a Person, not just truths. All Scripture points to Jesus's death and resurrection, to forgiveness, and to personal knowledge of God through him.

To profit from Scripture, one must take the right posture. At one extreme, the skeptic questions and judges whatever he or she reads. At the other, the overconfident believer, convinced that he has mastered biblical or systematic theology, ignores or explains away whatever fails to support his system. Interpreters should come to Scripture humbly, expecting to learn and be corrected and willing to observe Scripture closely and accept whatever they find. All Scripture is breathed out by God (2 Tim. 3:16), so every word counts. If a biblical narrator mentions something as seemingly insignificant as a character's hair, this detail will probably be important—as the hair of Esau, Samson, and Absalom shows!

Interpreters also need skills. The remainder of this chapter explains the skills necessary to read the Bible in context, to find the main point of a passage, to develop a theme, and to apply Scripture.

KNOWING THE CONTEXT

It is a truism that one must read the Bible in context, but the truism hides a distinction. "Context" can refer to the historical or the literary context. The *literary context* includes the words, sentences, and paragraphs preceding and following a passage. The literary context locates a passage within the larger purposes of a book. Readers should ask why a particular passage is *here* and not elsewhere, how it builds upon prior passages, and how it prepares for the next. The disciples once said to Jesus, "Increase our faith" (Luke 17:5). Absent a context, it seems like a godly request (which it may be in some contexts). But here the disciples say it after they hear a difficult command and before Jesus tells them they merely need the faith of a mustard seed. Considering this context, some interpreters have seen "Increase our faith" as an excuse, not a godly request.

One should also locate a passage in *the context of its entire book*. Paul's statement "I appeal to you therefore, brothers, by the mercies of God, to present your bodies as a living sacrifice, holy and acceptable to God . . ." (Rom. 12:1) stands at a hinge in Romans. Paul had just finished recounting God's mercies in Romans 3–11. His "therefore" summons readers to see that God's abundant mercies lead them into heartfelt service.

The *historical context* includes knowledge of the culture, economy, geography, climate, agriculture, architecture, family life, morals, and social structure of the Bible's actors, authors, and readers. Over the centuries, climate and topography hardly vary, but other factors shift more. For example, Israel was poor and weak under Samuel and Saul, strong and rich under David and Solomon.

Historical contexts help readers make sense of passages like Deuteronomy 22:8, which says a builder "shall make a parapet" around the roof of a new home, lest someone fall from it and "bring the guilt of blood" upon the house. A parapet is a retaining wall around the edge of a flat roof. Since Israelites worked, ate, and slept on their roofs, parapets kept reckless boys and restless sleepers from tumbling off. The law taught Israel how to preserve life and to love neighbors.

Again, in Luke 11:27–28 a woman called out to Jesus, "Blessed is the womb that bore you and the breasts at which you nursed." The woman's mind-set explains her odd-sounding speech. In antiquity, women gained honor by marrying a great man or bearing great children. The woman praised Jesus by praising his mother—only a great woman could bear such a great son. Jesus nudges her in another direction: "Blessed rather are those who hear the word of God and obey it." In other words, a woman finds greatness in discipleship more than in matrimony or maternity.

Interpreters must read carefully to recognize both obvious and hidden riddles. Some matters are less clear than they seem. Do contemporary readers know precisely what judges, elders, and talents are? Study resources include a study Bible, and also, in increasing depth, a Bible dictionary, an encyclopedia, and scholarly commentaries. The quality of sources, not the quantity, is paramount.

Background studies permit more accurate study of a text's line of thought. The genre of the passage must be noted, since narrative, law, prophecy, visions, wisdom literature, and epistles all have distinct modes of operation, with subtypes within each genre. To simplify, however, the most basic distinction in terms of genre is between *narrative* and *discourse*.

INTERPRETING NARRATIVES

Narratives can be long or short, complex or simple. They can be distinguished as speech stories, reports, and dramatic narratives. A speech story sets up a significant teaching, usually delivered near the end. Consider Jesus's encounters with a centurion (Matt. 8:5–13) and with Zacchaeus (Luke 19:1–10). Reports briefly describe battles, travels, or minor kings. They lack drama and reveal their secrets through patterns. For example, taken together, the reports of Solomon's reign show gold slowly becoming more prominent, and more highly valued, than wisdom. Solomon spent more on his palace than on the temple, and his adherence to the law steadily declined (1 Kings 4–11). Readers can draw conclusions as they read the reports in canonical perspective.

Many narratives feature complex characters and dramatic tension. To interpret narrative, one must note the story's time and place, its characters, and their interests. Soon conflict develops, leading to a crisis, then resolution. The reader should enter the story as if he or she were there, especially at the dramatic climax—when Abraham's knife is poised, when David strides toward Goliath. The resolution follows—the angel calls out, the stone finds its mark. Narratives convey moral, spiritual, and theological truths (1 Cor. 10:11), but one must first look for God's action. He is the prime character in biblical narratives. Readers should ask therefore how God reveals himself, and how he fulfills his covenant promises, in this or that particular story.

The main point of a narrative typically appears in the climax-resolution nexus. The narrator or a character in the story will often reveal that central truth. Dialogue discloses character and motivation (e.g., Luke 15:28–32). In the Abraham-Isaac account, both Abraham and the narrator say that the Lord will provide, and he does (Gen. 22:8, 14). In the David-Goliath narrative, David says, "The battle is the LORD's, and he will give you into our hand," and he does (1 Sam. 17:45–49). The main point in these narratives is not "Abraham obeyed a hard command and believers should, too," or "David was brave and Christians should be, too." The lessons are that "the Lord provides" and "the battle is the Lord's" (and then, also, that he is certainly worthy of trust!). The stories' characters go on quests, face choices, and respond to God faithfully or unfaithfully—but the Lord is the main agent, and believers, unbelievers, and bystanders are always responding to him. In the process they show how people tend to respond, for good or ill, and Bible readers should imitate their good responses and avoid their mistakes.

INTERPRETING DISCOURSE

In discourse, which is the other main type of text in the Bible, the search for the main point (not necessarily the point that most interests the reader) remains central as well. This is true whether the text is poetry, prophecy, or an epistle. The point commonly appears first or last in a passage. (Whole books also have themes that are stated first or last; see Matt. 28:18–20 and Rom. 1:16–17.) Many Psalms reveal their theme at once: "Bless the LORD, O my soul" (103:1; see also 42:1; 107:1). Passages in the Epistles sometimes start with the main point and then elaborate on it. James, for instance, says straight off that not many should aspire to be teachers (3:1a) because they face stricter judgment (3:1b) and because the tongue is beyond control (3:2–8). Other passages build to a climax, as in Jesus's teaching on the law, "You therefore must be perfect as your heavenly father is perfect" (Matt. 5:48). On numerous occasions, writers repeat the main point. The author of Judges says twice that "everyone did what was right in his own eyes" (17:6; 21:25). Paul tells the Corinthians three times to be content in their assigned calling (1 Cor. 7:17, 20, 24). Careful students of Scripture will reread a passage, both to find the main point and to observe the way the biblical authors think. Illustrations, elaborations, and answers to foes are best understood by seeing how they serve the principal lesson.

This is not to say that the main point should be considered the only point or the only important point. For example, though Romans 1:16–17 is the overall theme of Romans, literally hundreds of other theological and ethical truths are taught throughout the pages of this letter. The individual parts are best understood in light of how they contribute to the whole.

TRACING SPECIFIC THEMES THROUGHOUT THE BIBLE

Interpreters also need to learn how to search through Scripture to collect its comprehensive teaching on various specific themes. Students can start topical studies by reading passages listed in their Bibles' cross-references. Concordances are valuable, but they can mislead if readers simply limit their scope to verses that use a particular word. Students of the Bible must locate concepts, not just words, to develop a theme. For example, a concordance search on "pray/prayer/praying" would turn up only one verse in John's Gospel (John 17:9), but several other verses tell how to "ask" God for various things, and those verses also teach a number of particular lessons about prayer. Ideas also unfold progressively within the Old Testament, into the New Testament, and sometimes even within a single book. Wise interpreters still locate every verse in its context and ask how the original audience understood it. For great topics such as work, marriage, or the love of God, it helps to note what the Bible says within the frame of each of the four great epochs: creation, fall, redemption, and restoration.

APPLYING GOD'S WORD

Biblical application chiefly requires careful prayer and meditation, but one must realize that application is more than following commands. Applying Scripture means accepting and fulfilling God-given duties, seeking a godly character, pursuing goals that the Lord blesses, and seeing the world his way. This produces four questions readers can ask themselves that often lead to helpful application: What should I do? Who should I be (or who should I realize that I am, in Christ)? Where should I go? How can I see?

People also apply the Bible when they let it lead them to Christ. After the fall, the Lord promised a Redeemer. Every good prophet, priest, king, and judge points to One who would perfectly fulfill their roles, and every false leader causes the reader to cry out for One who would be true. From the start of the Gospels, Jesus is portrayed as Son of God and Son of Man. Each phase in the Gospel accounts leads toward the climax in the crucifixion and its resolution in the resurrection. Each epistle interprets that great event until Scripture ends in Revelation's songs of praise to the Lamb and the Lion, the King of kings and Lord of lords, contemplated, trusted, and adored. Thus interpretative skills must lead beyond conceptual knowledge to a Person, and a vital relationship with him.

2

INTERPRETING THE BIBLE: A HISTORICAL OVERVIEW

John Hannah

Is there any benefit to reading the Bible as it was understood by previous generations of Christians? Yes, certainly, because the Bible was written for them as well as us. God spoke to them through the Bible as he does to us today, and the spiritual gift of teaching was given to individuals then as it is now. Therefore when we read the biblical interpretations of previous generations, going all the way back to the earliest days of the church, we can often gain insight and perspectives that we might otherwise overlook because of the cultural biases of our own time.

However, before we seek to benefit from the interpretations of previous generations, it is helpful to have a broad overview of the dominant methods of biblical interpretation from various periods in church history.

The earliest followers of Christ interpreted the Hebrew Scriptures (the Old Testament) as Jesus taught them—as a book of anticipations pointing to Christ himself. He was the long-promised Messiah, the Redeemer who would reverse the effects of the primal fall and restore the world to pristine holiness. Jesus taught that the Old Testament spoke of him. To his critics he said, "You search the Scriptures because you think that in them you have eternal life; and it is they that bear witness about me" (John 5:39). The Gospel accounts suggest that Jesus understood the Old Testament from a christocentric, typological perspective; he is repeatedly cast as the fulfillment of the Scriptures. In the Sermon on the Mount, Jesus made it clear that his views did not contradict Moses, but that he had come to invest the Law and the Prophets with their proper and full meaning (Matt. 5:17). Two themes run through Jesus's teaching: (1) the Law was the perfect revelation of God to humanity, and (2) Jesus came to fulfill the Law by meeting its exacting demands for a righteous standing before God.

This approach to the Old Testament is how the earliest writers of the Christian Scriptures (the New Testament) approached their own writings. They spoke of the Old Testament in the same way that Jesus had: as a book not telling merely the pre-Christian history of Israel but telling that history in a way that had present and future significance for Christians. The Old Testament was the original sacred book of the church, giving assurance that Jesus was the promised and anointed one predicted by the prophets.

MARCION

Not everyone in the early church grasped the concept of continuity between the two Testaments, as evidenced by Marcion, who taught in Rome between AD 140 and 160. He argued that the Old Testament was vastly inferior to the writings of the apostles, most notably Paul's. Marcion adopted a literal approach to interpretation, but his dualistic grid discounted the Old Testament, which he believed set forth a different God from the Father of the Lord Jesus Christ, and was not to be read in the churches. His approach pitted law against grace, and the Old Testament God against a God of love. The wider church, however, soon recognized Marcion's innovations as a mistake.

JUSTIN MARTYR AND IRENAEUS

In reaction to Marcion, other Christian teachers formulated a more orthodox way of approaching the sacred writings. Justin Martyr (c. AD 100–165), an early defender of Christianity, argued that the difference between the Old Testament and New Testament is only a matter of degree. The Old Testament anticipated and foretold events, and was superseded by the New Testament writings because they represented the fulfillment of earlier anticipations. Thus, Justin Martyr, particularly in his *Dialogue*, stressed a messianic continuity and utilized a literal-historical approach to interpretation.

However, it was Irenaeus (c. AD 130–200) who gathered the threads of interpretation more systematically. Though his approach to the Old Testament was more literal than that of his predecessors, he also saw a typological meaning in the text. In Irenaeus's view the Scriptures are like "treasure hidden in a field" (Matt. 13:44) in that the literal was also the typological: the Bible is full of prefigurements, especially of the Messiah. Irenaeus also championed ideas that are still generally accepted by modern interpreters: (1) exegesis should pay careful attention to context; (2) unclear or obscure texts should be interpreted by clearer ones; and (3) a nonliteral reading of some passages may be warranted. Irenaeus held that the true meaning of the Scriptures is the interpretation of the apostles as presented in the New Testament and is embodied in the Rule of Faith (that is, the established and widely accepted understanding of the main doctrines of Scripture) as preserved through the teachings of the church.

CLEMENT AND ORIGEN

Christian teachers in Alexandria, such as Clement (c. AD 150–215) and Origen (c. 185–254), were profoundly influenced by the work of Philo (a Jewish philosopher who wrote, and thought, in Greek; d. 50) and Plato's philosophy of Idealism. Clement and Origen read the Bible as having multiple levels of meaning. The surface meaning was literal, but it often hid a deeper, spiritual meaning. They held the Bible to be verbally accurate, and in this manner the integrity of the text was preserved; but where the literal meaning was obscure, this was thought to suggest a more profound, allegorical meaning. To Origen, who systematized this newer approach, the literal or simple meaning of the text was for those who could not grasp the intricate nature of languages (i.e., figures of speech, mysterious sayings), while the deeper meaning was for the learned or more spiritual. Using the body-soul-spirit analogy, he argued that the Bible should be interpreted literally, morally, and mystically. As a result, the historical meaning of Scripture was devalued. The deep meaning of the text could be separated from the literal meaning, resulting in theological speculation. This approach, therefore, was marked by subjectivity, depending more upon the insight of the interpreter rather than seeking consistency with other established doctrines of Scripture. Though Origen never contradicted the Rule of Faith, he did in fact speculate beyond it.

THEODORE, JEROME, AND AUGUSTINE

Later teachers such as Theodore of Mopsuestia (c. AD 350–428), Jerome (c. 342–420), and Augustine (354–430) criticized the allegorical method of the Alexandrians as being arbitrary and nonrational. These teachers argued that the Scriptures are to be interpreted in both a literal and a christocentric sense. They insisted that their method was not the same as the allegorical approach, because it was rooted in the text of Scripture itself. They refused to disconnect the literal, historical meaning of the text from its spiritual meaning. Jerome, though initially a proponent of allegorization, later embraced the literal-historical approach to Scripture without abandoning the deeper spiritual meaning of the text that had been championed by Theodore and others. Jerome insisted that scriptural texts should be read in a historical context, something the allegorical approach had de-emphasized.

The greatest theologian of the early church was Augustine. He championed a literal, historical approach to reading the Bible, insisting that a proper understanding must begin with the mind of the writer, which required knowing the biblical languages and paying attention to context. The fourfold approach to Scripture that he put forth (see below) was widely used, and abused, in the Medieval era.

MEDIEVAL CHURCHMEN

The Medieval church gradually became enamored of the allegorical method of interpretation, which was used to buttress church dogma that lacked a strong basis in Scripture. Medievalists developed a fourfold approach to interpreting the Bible: the *literal*, showing what God did; the *allegorical*, showing what at surface level God hid; the *moral*, revealing what believers should do; and the *mystical*, or *anagogical*, showing the heavenly life in which, for Christians, things will end. In effect, the method obscured the true meaning of the Bible by imposing arbitrary meanings on it. Theology took precedence over careful literal-historical exegesis.

In the high Middle Ages, the great scholastic Thomas Aquinas (1225–1274) embraced the literal-historical (as opposed to allegorical) approach. In his skillful hands the proper approach to the Bible was an exegetical method that assumed the primacy of the literal meaning of the text. To Aquinas, multiplying levels of meaning in a single text was confusing in that it would blunt the force of any biblical argument; further, he thought that a parabolic sense of Scripture could be part of its proper meaning.

He recognized that the intended meaning of a text is contained in words, and words can be used both literally (in a narrow sense, excluding images and metaphors) and figuratively.

THE REFORMERS

The Protestant Reformers of the sixteenth century reacted against the misuse of the Bible in Late Medieval theology. They insisted that authority rested not in the leaders or fathers of the church but in a proper understanding of the text derived from correct methods of literary interpretation. Reformers starting with John Wycliffe (c. 1330–1384) insisted on a grammatical-historical approach to the Bible. The German reformer Martin Luther (1483–1546) broke with the nonliteral, allegorical approach that was dominant in his training and returned to the patristic emphasis on the centrality of Christ in the Scriptures. He was adamant that the Bible be approached not through fanciful allegories or merely to support established dogma but through ordinary language and literal, historical, and grammatical exegesis. A proper understanding of the Bible should be the product of such interpretation of the scriptural texts and should lead to healthy theology and a robust Christian life.

The most prolific expositor of Scripture, as well as the first major systematizer of Protestant theology, was John Calvin (1509–1564). Calvin stressed Scripture over theology and saw theology as the fruit resulting from the proper interpretation of Scripture. He was a skilled linguist who approached the Bible from the viewpoint of its historical veracity, literal interpretation, and contextual analysis. He often interpreted prophetic texts in a typological manner (as looking forward to Christ), yet he strenuously opposed arbitrary allegorization, which he believed undermined the certainty and clarity of Scripture. Some assign to Calvin the designation "the founder of modern grammatical-historical exegesis," which is confirmed by the continued popularity of his commentaries and the way in which modern interpreters still interact with him as a sober, accurate exegete.

THE ENLIGHTENMENT

In the generations following Calvin, the role of tradition in biblical interpretation was increasingly limited by a growing emphasis on the individual interpreter, a trend seen in the rise of the Enlightenment. (The Renaissance led to two great movements: the *Protestant Reformation*, which emancipated the Bible from ecclesiastical imprisonment, and the *Enlightenment*, which carried forward the attack on authority structures to ridicule the authority of the Bible, birthing the Modern era.) The essence of the Enlightenment was a rejection of the biblical doctrine of the utter brokenness of humanity and a belief that the human mind was capable of arriving at truth when unhindered by external authorities such as the church, tradition, or the Bible.

To many Enlightenment thinkers, the Bible became an untrustworthy book created by churchmen to keep minds captive under the threat of punishment. Thus, in the eighteenth and nineteenth centuries, university scholarship embraced the intellectual and philosophical assumptions of the Enlightenment, turning its full force against the veracity of the Scriptures. The Bible became viewed as a parched landscape with an occasional oasis. At best, it merely contained truth; it was not itself truth. The lasting effects of this approach have contributed to the dissolution of the Christian worldview, at least in Western industrialized nations.

THE HEIRS OF THE REFORMATION: EVANGELICAL PROTESTANTISM

However, from the Reformation until today, the large central core of the Protestant church worldwide has held to an "evangelical" view of Scripture, rejecting the skepticism of post-Enlightenment Naturalism and Rationalism, and continuing to believe in the complete truthfulness and reliability of the Bible. In answer to the attacks of rationalism, evangelicals have shown that there is no contradiction between full trust in the Bible and intellectual integrity. With respect to proper biblical interpretation, they have appreciated the various understandings of Scripture held by previous generations but have also sought to correct previous misunderstandings by developing more precise standards for right interpretation (see chap. 1).

CONCLUSION

After centuries of the most rigorous scrutiny, the Bible is still the most widely read book in the world. The God of the Scriptures has preserved his divine Word—recorded in human language and illumined by the Spirit. This Word reveals the Savior of the world to the hungry hearts who affectionately embrace him and walk in his ways. Some may argue that the Bible is not true, yet the Holy Scriptures will remain an eternal testimony to God's truthfulness long after the last critic is silenced. While not perfect, the long history of interpretation by those who read the Bible as God's Word in previous centuries is still a storehouse of great riches for modern readers. Because the Bible uses ordinary language and teaches through concepts and experiences common to all human life, interpreters of previous centuries often were accurate in their understanding of vast parts of Scripture. For those who will read the Bible in light of this long tradition (yet correcting and supplementing that tradition's inadequacies), it promises to reveal the truth of a divine Redeemer and to instruct us in walking humbly before him in reverence and awe.

Part 2

READING THE BIBLE

3

READING THE BIBLE THEOLOGICALLY

J. I. Packer

To read the Bible "theologically" means to read the Bible with a focus on God: his being, his character, his words and works, his purpose, presence, power, promises, and precepts. The Bible can be read from different standpoints and with different centers of interest, but this chapter seeks to explain how to read it theologically.

THE BIBLE: THE CHURCH'S INSTRUCTION BOOK

All sixty-six books of the Bible constitute the book of the Christian church. And the church, both as a whole and in the life of its members, must always be seen to be the people of the book. This glorifies God, its primary author.

God has chosen to restore his sin-spoiled world through a long and varied historical process, central to which is the creating—by redemptive and sanctifying grace—of what is literally a new human race. This unfinished process has so far extended over four millennia. It began with Abraham; it centers on the first coming of the incarnate Lord, Jesus Christ; and it is not due for completion till he comes again. Viewed as a whole, from the vantage point of God's people within it, the process always was and still is covenantal and educative. *Covenantal* indicates that God says to his gathered community, "I am your God; you shall be my people," and with his call for loyalty he promises them greater future good than any they have yet known. *Educative* indicates that, within the covenant, God works to change each person's flawed and degenerate nature into a new, holy selfhood that expresses in responsive terms God's own moral likeness. The model is Jesus Christ, the only perfect being that the world has ever seen. For God's people to sustain covenantal hopes and personal moral ideals as ages pass and cultures change and decay, they must have constant, accessible, and authoritative instruction from God. And that is what the Bible essentially is.

This is why, in addition to equipping everywhere a class of teachers who will give their lives to inculcating Bible truth, the church now seeks to translate the Bible into each person's primary language and to spread universal literacy, so that all may read and understand it.

THE BIBLE IS CANONICAL

God's plan is that through his teaching embodied in the Bible, plus knowledge and experience of how he rewards obedience and punishes disobedience in a disciplinary way, his people should learn love, worship, and service of God himself, and love, care, and service of others, as exemplified by Jesus Christ. To this end each generation needs a written "textbook" that sets forth for all time God's unchanging standards of truth, right, love and goodness, wisdom and worship, doctrine and devotion. This resource will enable people to see what they should think and do, what ideals they should form, what goals they should set, what limits they should observe, and what life strategies they should follow. These are the functions that are being claimed for the Bible when it is called "canonical." A "canon" is a rule or a standard. The Bible is to be read as a God-given rule of belief and behavior—that is, of faith and life.

THE BIBLE IS INSPIRED

Basic to the Bible's canonical status is its "inspiration." This word indicates a divinely effected uniqueness comparable to the uniqueness of the person of the incarnate Lord. As Jesus Christ was totally human and totally divine, so is the Bible. All Scripture is witness to God, given by divinely illuminated human writers, and all Scripture is God witnessing to himself in and through their words. The way into the mind of God is through the expressed mind of these human writers, so the reader of the Bible looks for that characteristic first. But the text must be read, or reread, as God's own self-revelatory instruction, given in the form of this human testimony. In this way God tells the reader the truth about himself; his work past, present, and future; and his will for people's lives.

THE BIBLE IS UNIFIED

Basic also to the Bible's canonical status is the demonstrable unity of its contents. Scripture is no ragbag of religious bits and pieces, unrelated to each other; rather, it is a tapestry in which all the complexities of the weave display a single pattern of judgment and mercy, promise and fulfillment. The Bible consists of two separate collections: the Old Testament, written over a period of about one thousand years, and the New Testament, written within a generation several centuries after the Old Testament was completed. Within such a composite array one would

31

expect to find some crossed wires or incoherence, but none are found here. While there are parallel narratives, repetitions, and some borrowings from book to book, the Bible as a whole tells a single, straightforward story. God the Creator is at the center throughout; his people, his covenant, his kingdom, and its coming king are the themes unfolded by the historical narratives, while the realities of redemption from sin and of godly living (faith, repentance, obedience, prayer, adoration, hope, joy, and love) become steadily clearer. Jesus Christ, as fulfiller of Old Testament prophecies, hopes, promises, and dreams, links the two Testaments together in an unbreakable bond. Aware that at the deepest level the whole Bible is the product of a single mind, the mind of God, believers reading it theologically always look for the inner links that bind the books together. And they are there to be found.

THEOLOGICAL READING OF THE BIBLE: A QUEST FOR GOD

Reading Scripture theologically starts from the truths reviewed above: (1) that the Bible is a God-given guide to sinners for their salvation, and for the life of grateful godliness to which salvation calls them; (2) that the Bible is equally the church's handbook for worship and service; (3) that it is a divinely inspired unity of narrative and associated admonition, a kind of running commentary on the progress of God's kingdom plan up to the establishing of a world-embracing, witnessing, suffering church in the decades following Christ's ascension and the Pentecost outpouring of the Spirit; and (4) that the incarnate Son of God himself, Jesus the Christ, crucified, risen, glorified, ministering, and coming again, is the Bible's central focus, while the activities of God's covenant people both before and after Christ's appearing make up its ongoing story. Theological reading follows these leads and is pursued theocentrically, looking and listening for God throughout, with the controlling purpose of discerning him with maximum clarity, through his own testimony to his will, works, and ways. Such reading is pursued prayerfully, according to Martin Luther's observation that the first thing one needs to become a theologian through Bible reading is prayer for the illumination and help of the Holy Spirit. And prayerful theological Bible reading will be pursued in light of three further guiding principles.

First, *revelation was progressive.* Its progress, in its written form, was not (as has sometimes been thought) from fuzzy and sometimes false (Old Testament) to totally true and clear (New Testament), but from partial to full and complete. "Long ago, at many times and in many ways, God spoke to our fathers by the prophets, but in these last days [the concluding era of this world's life] he has spoken to us by his Son" (Heb. 1:1–2). In the Gospels, the Epistles, and the books of Acts and Revelation, readers are now faced with God's final word to the world before Christ comes again. Theological Bible reading maintains this perspective, traversing the Old Testament by the light of the New Testament.

Second, *the Bible's God-language is analogical.* Today's fashion is to call it "metaphorical," which is not wrong, but "analogical" is the term that makes clearest the key point: the difference involved when everyday words—nouns, verbs, adjectives—are used of God. Language is God's gift for personal communication between humans and between God and humans. But when God speaks of himself—or when people speak to him or about him—the definitions, connotations, implications, valuations, and range of meaning in each case must be adjusted in light of the differences between him and his creation. God is infinite and flawless; people are both finite and flawed. So when everyday words are used of God, all thought of finiteness and imperfection must be removed, and the overall notion of unlimited, self-sustaining existence in perfect loving holiness must be added in. For instance, when God calls himself "Father," or his people in response call him their "Father," the thought will be of authoritative, protecting, guiding, and enriching love, free from any lack of wisdom that appears in earthly fathers. And when one speaks of God's "anger" or "wrath" in retribution for sin that he as the world's royal Judge displays, the thought will be as free from the fitful inconsistency, irrationality, bad temper, and loss of self-control that regularly mars human anger.

These mental adjustments underlie the biblical insistence that all God's doings, even those that involve human distress, are glorious and praiseworthy. This doxological, God-glorifying tone and thrust marks even books such as Job and Lamentations, and the many complaint prayers in the Psalter. The Bible writers practice analogical adjustment so smoothly, unobtrusively, and unselfconsciously that it is easy to overlook what they are doing. But the theological reader of the Bible will not miss this point.

Third, *the one God of the Bible is Trinitarian and triune.* God is three persons in an eternal fellowship of love and cooperation within the one divine Being. Each person is involved in all that God does. God is a team no less than he is a complex entity. In the New Testament this concept is apparent, but in the Old Testament, where the constant emphasis is on the truth that Yahweh is the one and only God, the truth of the Trinity hardly breaks the surface. God's triunity is, however, an eternal fact, though it has been clearly revealed only through Christ's coming. Theological Bible readers are right to read this fact back into the Old Testament, following the example of New Testament writers in their citing of many Old Testament passages.

THEOLOGICAL READING OF THE BIBLE: THE QUEST FOR GODLINESS

Theology is for doxology, that is, glorifying God by praise and thanks, by obedient holiness, and by laboring to extend God's kingdom, church, and cultural influence. The goal of theological Bible reading is not just to know truth about God (though one's quest for godliness must start there) but to know God personally in a relationship that honors him—which means serving Jesus Christ, the Father's Son, the world's real though unrecognized Lord, who came to earth, died, rose, and ascended for his people, and has given them the Holy Spirit. To have him fill believers' horizons and rule their lives in his Father's name is the authentic form—the foundation, blueprint, scaffolding, and construction— of Christian godliness, to which theological Bible reading is a God-intended means. So, three questions must govern readers of the inspired Word:

First, in the passage being read, *what is shown about God the Father, Son, and Holy Spirit?* What does it say about what the holy Three are doing, have done, and will do in God's world, in his church, and in lives committed to him? What does it reveal about God's attributes, that is, God's power and character, how he exists and how he behaves? One reason, no doubt, for God's panoramic, multigenred layout of the Bible—with history, homily, biography, liturgy, practical philosophy, laws, lists, genealogies, visions, and so on, all rubbing shoulders—is that this variety provides so many angles of illumination on these questions for theological Bible readers' instruction.

Second, in the passage being read, *what is shown about the bewildering, benighted world with all its beautiful and beneficial aspects alongside those that are corrupt and corrupting?* Discerning the world's good and evil for what they are, so as to embrace the world's good and evade its temptations, is integral to the godliness that theological Bible reading should promote.

Third, in the passage being read, *what is shown to guide one's living, this day and every day?* The theological logic of this question, through which the reader must work each time, is this: since God, by his own testimony, said *that* to those people in their situation, what does it follow that he says to readers today in their own situation? The Holy Spirit answers prayer by giving discernment to apply Scripture in this way. Those who seek will indeed find.

4

READING THE BIBLE
AS LITERATURE

Leland Ryken

Three primary modes of writing converge in the Bible: theological, historical, and literary. Overwhelmingly, theology
and history are embodied in literary form.

A crucial principle of interpretation thus needs to be established at the outset: meaning is communicated *through form*,
starting with the very words of a text but reaching beyond that
to considerations of literary genre and style. We cannot properly
speak about the theological or moral content of a story or poem
(for example) without first interacting with the story or poem.

Literary form exists prior to content; no content exists apart
from the form in which it is embodied. As a result, the first
responsibility of a reader or interpreter is to understand the form
of a discourse. It is a common misconception to think that the
literary dimension of the Bible is *only* the form in which the mes-

sage is presented. Actually, without some kind of literary form, the content would not even exist. The concept of literary form needs to be construed very broadly here. Anything having to do with *how* a biblical author has expressed his message constitutes literary form. We tend to think (erroneously) that authors tell us *about* characters, actions, and situations, whereas actually they speak *with* or *by means of* these things—*about* God, people, and the world.

THE BIBLE AS LITERATURE
The idea of the Bible as literature began with the Bible itself. The writers refer to a whole range of literary genres in which they write: proverb, saying, chronicle, complaint (lament psalm), oracle, apocalypse, parable, song, epistle, and many others. Some of these forms correspond to the literary forms current in the authors' surrounding cultures. For example, the Ten Commandments are cast in the form of the suzerainty treaties that ancient Near Eastern kings imposed on their subjects, and the New Testament epistles show many affinities to the structure of Greek and Roman letters of the same era.

Mainly, though, we can look to the Bible itself to see the extent to which it is a literary book. Virtually every page of the Bible is replete with literary technique, and to possess the individual texts fully, we need to read the Bible as literature, just as we need to read it theologically and (in the narrative parts) historically.

LITERARY GENRES
The most customary way to define literature is by the external genres (types or kinds of writing) in which its content is expressed. The two main genres in the Bible are narrative and poetry. Numerous categories cluster under each of these. Narrative subtypes, for example, include hero story, gospel, epic,

tragedy, comedy (a U-shaped plot with a happy ending), and parable. Specific poetic genres keep multiplying as well: lyric, lament psalm, praise psalm, love poem, nature poem, *epithalamion* (wedding poem), and many others.

But those are only the tip of the iceberg. In addition to narrative and poetry, we find prophecy, visionary writing, apocalypse, pastoral, encomium, oratory, drama (the book of Job), satire, and epistle. Then if we add more specific forms like travel story, dramatic monologue, doom song, and Christ hymn, the number of literary genres in the Bible readily exceeds a hundred.

The importance of genre to biblical interpretation is that genres have their own methods of procedure and rules of interpretation. An awareness of genre should alert us to what we can expect to find in a text. Additionally, considerations of genre should govern the terms in which we interact with a text. With narrative, for example, we are on the right track if we pay attention to plot, setting, and character. If the text before us is a satire, we need to think in terms of object of attack, the satiric vehicle in which the attack is couched, and satiric norm (stated or implied standard by which the criticism is being conducted).

In view of how many literary genres are present in the Bible, it is obvious that the overall literary form of the Bible is the anthology, as even the word Bible (Gk. *biblia*, "books") hints. As an anthology, the Bible possesses the same kinds of unity that other anthologies exhibit: multiple authorship (approximately three dozen authors), diverse genres, a rationale for collecting these particular materials (a unifying religious viewpoint and story of salvation history), comprehensiveness, and an identifiable strategy of organization (a combination of historical chronology and groupings by genre).

LITERARY SUBJECT MATTER

Literature is also identifiable by its subject matter. It is differentiated from expository (informational) writing by the way in which it presents concrete human experience instead of stating abstract propositions, logical arguments, or bare facts. We can profitably think of biblical writing as existing on a continuum, with abstract propositional discourse on one end and concrete presentation of human experience on the other. The more thoroughly a piece of writing falls on the experiential end of the spectrum, the more "literary" it is.

To illustrate, the command "you shall not murder" is an example of expository discourse. The story of Cain and Abel embodies the same truth in the form of characters in concrete settings performing physical and mental actions. Expository writing gives us the precept; literature gives us the example. "God's provision extends to all aspects of our lives" is a thematic summary of Psalm 23; rather than such abstraction, however, the psalm incarnates the truth about providence through the poetic image of a shepherd's daily routine with his sheep.

The subject of literature is human experience rendered as concretely as possible. The result is that it possesses a universal quality. Whereas history and the daily news tell us what *happened*, literature tells us what *happens*—what is true for all people in all places and times. A text can be both informational and literary, but its literary dimension resides in its embodiment of recognizable human experience.

The goal of literature is to prompt a reader vicariously to share or relive an experience. The truth that literature imparts is not simply ideas that are true but *truthfulness to human experience*. The implication for interpreting the Bible as literature is that readers and expositors need to actively recreate experiences in their imaginations, identify the recognizable human experiences in a text (thereby building bridges to life in the modern world), and resist the impulse immediately to reduce every biblical passage to a set of theological ideas.

ARCHETYPES AND MOTIFS

An archetype is a plot motif (such as initiation or quest), character type (such as the villain or trickster), or image (such as light or water) that recurs throughout literature and life. The presence of archetypes signals a text's literary quality. When we read literature, we are continuously aware of such archetypes as the temptation motif, the dangerous valley, and the hero, whereas with other types of writing we are rarely aware of archetypes.

Archetypes are the building blocks of literature. The Bible is the most complete repository of archetypes in the Western world, something that makes the Bible universal, reaching down to bedrock human experience. Awareness of archetypes helps us see the unity of the Bible (since we keep relating one instance of an archetype to other instances), and also the connections between the Bible and other literature.

STYLISTICS AND RHETORIC

Literature also uses distinctive resources of language that set it apart from ordinary expository discourse. The most obvious example is poetry. Poets speak a language all their own, consisting of images and figures of speech. Other important examples include: imagery, metaphor, simile, symbol, allusion, irony, wordplay, hyperbole, apostrophe (direct address to someone or something absent as though present), personification, paradox, and pun. The presence of these elements push a text into the category of literature.

The most concentrated repository of such language in the Bible is the books that are poetic in their basic format—the Prophetic Books, Job, Psalms, Proverbs, Ecclesiastes (a book of prose poems), Song of Solomon, and Revelation. But literary resources of language also appear on virtually every page of the Bible beyond the poetic books—most obviously in the discourses of Jesus and in the Epistles, but less pervasively in the narratives as well.

A related literary phenomenon is rhetoric—arrangement of content in patterns and use of conventional literary techniques or formulas. Parallelism of sentence elements, for example, is an instance of stylized rhetoric. Patterns of repetition—of words, phrases, or content units—are a distinguishing feature of the Bible. So is aphoristic conciseness that continuously raises the Bible to a literary realm of eloquence far above everyday discourse. A page from a New Testament epistle might include rhetorical questions, question-and-answer constructions, direct addresses to real or imaginary respondents, or repeated words or phrases.

ARTISTRY

Literature is an art form in which beauty of expression, craftsmanship, and verbal virtuosity are valued as self-rewarding and as an enhancement of effective communication. The writer of Ecclesiastes states his philosophy of composition, portraying himself as a self-conscious stylist and wordsmith who arranged his material "with great care" and who "sought to find words of delight" (Eccles. 12:9–10). Surely other biblical writers did the same.

The standard elements of artistic form include unity, theme-and-variation, pattern, design, progression, contrast, balance, recurrence, coherence, and symmetry. Authors cultivate artistry because it is important to their effect and intention. The Bible is an aesthetic as well as utilitarian book, and we need to experience it as such.

READING AND INTERPRETING THE BIBLE AS LITERATURE

Any piece of writing needs to be interpreted in terms of the kind of writing that it is. The Bible is a literary book in which theology and history are usually embodied in literary forms. Those forms include genres, the incarnation of human experience in concrete form, stylistic and rhetorical techniques, and artistry.

These literary features are not extraneous aspects of the text. Instead, they are the forms *through which* the content is mediated. If the writing of the Bible is the product of divine inspiration—if it represents what the Holy Spirit prompted the authors to write as they were "carried along" (2 Pet. 1:21)—then the literary forms of the Bible have also been inspired by God and need to be granted an importance congruent with that inspiration.

5

READING THE BIBLE IN PRAYER AND COMMUNION WITH GOD

John Piper

Communion with God is a staggering thought. God created billions of galaxies and calls every star by name (Isa. 40:26; 42:5). He never had a beginning and will never end (Ps. 90:2). His ways are inscrutable and his judgments unsearchable (Rom. 11:33). His thoughts are as different from ours as the heavens are high above the earth (Isa. 55:8). "The nations are like a drop from a bucket, and are accounted as the dust on the scales" (Isa. 40:15).

If that were not enough to make communion with God unthinkable, consider that all of us are naturally rebellious against him. Therefore, his omnipotent wrath rests on us. We are by nature hostile to God and do not submit to his law (Rom. 8:7). Therefore, the wrath of God is revealed from heaven against us (Rom. 1:18). We are "by nature children of wrath," "sons of

disobedience," and "dead in . . . trespasses and sins" (Eph. 2:1–5).
How then can there be any thought of communion with God?

FOR OUR JOY

Before we see the Bible's answer, let's clarify what we mean by
"communion." Communion refers to God's communication and
presentation of himself to us, together with our proper response
to him with joy. We say "with joy" because it would not be communion if God revealed himself in total wrath and we were simply
terrified. That would be *true* revelation and a *proper* response,
but it would not be communion.

Communion assumes that God comes to us in love and that
we respond joyfully to the beauty of his perfections and the
offer of his fellowship. He may sometimes come with a rod of
discipline. But even in our tears, we can rejoice in our Father's
loving discipline (Heb. 12:6–11). Communion with God may
lay us in ashes or make us leap. But it never destroys our joy. It
is our joy (Ps. 43:4).

TO GOD'S GLORY

Communion with God is the end for which we were created. The
Bible says that we were created for the glory of God (Isa. 43:7).
Yet glorifying God is not something we do *after* communing
with him, but *by* communing with him. Many human deeds
magnify the glory of God's goodness, but only if they flow from
our contentment in communion with him. This is why we pray,
"*Satisfy us* in the morning with your steadfast love" (Ps. 90:14).
The joy of this communion in the love of God confirms God's
worth and shows his glory.

BECAUSE OF THE GOSPEL

But how is this unthinkable privilege of communion with God
possible for sinners like us? The answer of the Bible is that God

himself took the initiative to be reconciled to his enemies. He sent his Son, Jesus Christ, to die in our place and bear the curse that we deserved from God. "Christ redeemed us from the curse of the law by becoming a curse for us" (Gal. 3:13). So the wrath of God that we deserved fell on Christ (Isa. 53:4–6, 10).

Because God gave Christ as our substitute, we can be reconciled to God and enjoy peaceful communion with him. "While we were enemies we were reconciled to God by the death of his Son" (Rom. 5:10). "Therefore, since we have been justified by faith, we have peace with God through our Lord Jesus Christ" (Rom. 5:1). This peace leads to the unparalleled joy of communion with God (Rom. 5:11).

THE GOSPEL: THE BIBLE'S CENTRAL MESSAGE

Therefore, the first thing to say about the Bible in relation to communion with God is that the message of how to be reconciled to God for the glory of God is the central message of the Bible. There is no communion with God without salvation from *our* sin and *God's* wrath. The Bible is the only book with final authority that tells us what God did through Christ and how we must respond through faith to be saved and to enjoy communion with God (2 Tim. 3:15).

But the Bible is more. The Bible tells the story of creation, of the fall of humanity into sin, and of the history of God's chosen people Israel leading up to the coming of the Messiah, Jesus. Then it recounts the life of Christ and his teachings, his mighty works, his death, his resurrection, and his ascension. Finally, it tells the story of the early church after Jesus had returned to heaven, and how we are to live until Jesus comes again.

THE BIBLE REVEALS GOD

The God-inspired record of this history (the Bible) is the only infallible and authoritative book communicating and presenting God himself (2 Tim. 3:16–17; 2 Pet. 1:21). To be sure, God is active everywhere in the world today, and we experience his precious power wherever we trust him and do his will. But we will go astray if we make this daily experience of God the basis of our communion with him. We know God for who he is, and meet him as he is, when we meet him through his Word—the Bible. We see this principle at work, for example, in 1 Samuel 3:21: "The LORD revealed *himself* to Samuel at Shiloh by the *word* of the LORD." The Lord *himself* is revealed by his *word*, that is, by what he *says* to us, whether audibly or in written form.

Therefore, when we seek to enjoy communion with the Lord—and not to be led astray by the ambiguities of religious experience—we read the Bible. From Genesis to Revelation, God's words and God's deeds reveal God himself for our knowledge and our enjoyment. Of course, it is possible to read the Bible without enjoying communion with God. We must seek to understand the Bible's meaning, and we must pause to contemplate what we understand and, by the Spirit, to feel and express the appropriate response of the heart.

God communicates with us in many ways through the Bible and seeks the response of our communion with him. If God indicts us (2 Cor. 7:8–10), we respond to him with sorrow and repentance. If he commends us (Ps. 18:19–20), we respond to him with humble gratitude and joy. If he commands us to do something (Matt. 28:19–20), we look to him for strength and resolve to obey with his help. If he makes a promise (Heb. 13:5–6), we marvel at his grace and trust him to do what he says. If he warns us of some danger (Luke 21:34), we take him seriously and watch with a thankful sense of his presence and protection. If he describes something about himself (Isa. 46:9–11), his Son (Mark 1:11), or his Holy Spirit (John 16:13–14), we affirm it and admire it and pray for clearer eyes to see and enjoy his greatness and beauty.

FELLOWSHIP WITH THE TRIUNE GOD

In all these communications, it is God himself that we most want to see. Communion with God is not merely *learning about* God but enjoying *fellowship with* God in the truth he reveals about himself. The apostle John, who enjoyed unusually close communion with Jesus while he was on the earth, said that he wrote his letters so that we might enjoy this fellowship: "That which we have seen and heard we proclaim also to you, so that you too may have fellowship with us; and indeed our fellowship is with the Father and with his Son Jesus Christ" (1 John 1:3). In other words, the Bible records the words and deeds of God so that by means of these we have fellowship—that is, communion—with God.

This fellowship is with each person in the Trinity: with the Father (1 John 1:3), with the Son (1 Cor. 1:9), and with the Holy Spirit (2 Cor. 13:14). This is possible because each person of the Godhead communicates with us in a way that corresponds to his unique role in creation, providence, and salvation. As the great Puritan John Owen wrote in his classic *Communion with God*, the Father communicates himself to us by the way of "original authority," the Son from a "purchased treasury," and the Spirit by an "immediate efficacy." Each person, as Owen says, communicates with us "distinctly" in the sense that we may discern from which person particular realizations of the grace of God come to us. But "distinctly" does not mean "separately": particular fellowship with each person of the Trinity is always one facet of ongoing communion with all three.

HUMBLE, BOLD PRAYER

Finally, from this Father-initiated, Son-purchased, Spirit-effected communion with God, we *pray* with humble boldness (Heb. 4:16). That is, we speak to God the Father, on the basis of Christ's work, by the help of the Spirit. This speaking is called *prayer*. It includes our confessions of sin (1 John 1:9), our praises of God's perfections (Ps. 96:4), our thanks for God's gifts (Ps. 118:21), and our requests that he would help us (Ps. 38:22) and others (Rom. 15:30–31)—all to the glory of God (Ps. 50:15), for the hallowing of his name, which must ever be our goal.

Prayer is the verbal aspect of our response to God in communion with him. The Bible does speak of "groanings too deep for words" (Rom. 8:26), but ordinarily prayer is the response of our heart to God in words. It may be in private (Matt. 6:6) or in public (1 Cor. 14:16). It may last all night (Luke 6:12) or be summed up in a moment's cry (Matt. 14:30). It may be desperate (Jonah 2:2) or joyful (Ps. 119:162). It may be full of faith (Mark 11:24) or wavering with uncertainty (Mark 9:24).

But it is not optional. It is commanded—which is good news, because it means that God loves being the giver of omnipotent help (Ps. 50:15). The Bible reminds us that ordinary people can accomplish great things by prayer (James 5:17–18). It tells us about great answers to prayer (Isa. 37:21, 36). It gives us great examples of how to pray (Matt. 6:9–13; Eph. 3:14–19). And it offers amazing encouragements to pray (Matt. 7:7–11).

GOD GETS THE GLORY; WE GET THE JOY

The Bible shows that prayer is near the heart of why God created the world. When we pray for God to do what only he can do, he alone gets the glory, while we get the joy. We see this when Jesus says, "Whatever you ask in my name, this I will do, *that the Father may be glorified* in the Son" (John 14:13), and then later says, "Ask, and you will receive, *that your joy may be full*" (John 16:24). In prayer, God gets the *glory* and we get the *joy*. God is the overflowing fountain; we are satisfied with the living water. He is infinitely rich; we are the happy heirs.

Central to all our praying, as we have seen, must be our longing that God's name be hallowed in the world—known and honored and loved (Matt. 6:9). To that end, we pray (1) for his church to be "filled with the fruit of righteousness . . . to the glory and praise of God" (Phil. 1:11); (2) that the gospel would spread and awaken faith in Jesus among all the nations (2 Thess. 3:1); and (3) that many who do not believe would be saved (Rom. 10:1). In this way, the aim of God's Word and the aim of prayer become the same: the glory of God and the salvation of the nations through Jesus Christ.

6

READING THE BIBLE FOR PERSONAL APPLICATION

David Powlison

It is a marvel how personally the Bible applies. The words pointedly address the concerns of long-ago people in faraway places, facing specific problems, many of which no longer exist. They had no difficulty seeing the application. Much of what they read *was* personal application to actual situations they were facing. But nothing in the Bible was written directly to you or specifically about what you face. We are reading someone else's mail. Yet the Bible repeatedly affirms that these words are also written for us: "Whatever was written in former days was written for our instruction" (Rom. 15:4; see also Deut. 29:29; 1 Cor. 10:11; 2 Tim. 3:15–17). Application today discovers ways in which the Spirit reapplies Scripture in a timely fashion.

Furthermore, the Bible is primarily about God, not you. The essential subject matter is the triune Redeemer Lord, culminating in Jesus Christ. When Jesus "opened their minds to understand the Scriptures" (Luke 24:45), he showed how everything written—creation, promises, commands, history, sacrificial system, psalms, proverbs—reveals him. We are reading someone else's biography. Yet that very story demonstrates how he includes us within his story. Jesus *is* the Word of God applied, all-wisdom embodied. As his disciples, we learn to similarly apply the Bible, growing up into his image. Application today experiences how the Spirit "rescripts" our lives by teaching us who God is and what he is doing.

"Personal application" proves wise when you reckon with these marvels. The Bible was written to others—but speaks to you. The Bible is about God—but draws you in. Your challenge is always to *reapply* Scripture afresh, because God's purpose is always to *rescript* your life. How can you expand your wisdom in personal application? The following four ways are suggested.

1. CONSOLIDATE WHAT YOU HAVE ALREADY LEARNED

Assuming that you have listened well to some parts of the Bible, consider these personal questions. What chunk of Scripture has made the most difference in your life? What verse or passage have you turned to most frequently? What makes these exact words frequently and immediately relevant? Your answer will likely embody four foundational truths about how to read the Bible for wise application.

First, this passage becomes your own because you listen. You remember what God says. He is saying this to you. You need these words. This promise, revelation, or command *must* be true. You *must* act on this call to faith and love. When you forget, you drift, stray, and flounder. When you remember and put it to work, bright truth rearranges your life. The foundation of application is always attentive listening to what God says.

Second, the passage and your life become fused. It is not simply a passage in the Bible. A specific word from God connects to some pointed struggle inside you and around you. These inner and outer troubles express your experience of the dual evil that plagues every human heart: sin and confusion from within; trouble and beguilement from without (1 Kings 8:37–39; Eccles. 9:3). But something God says invades your darkness with his light. He meets your actual need with his actual mercies. Your life and God's words meet. Application depends on honesty about where you need help. Your kind of trouble is everywhere in the Bible.

Third, your appropriation of this passage reveals how God himself does the applying. He meets you before you meet him. The passage arrested you. God arranged your struggle with sin and suffering so that you would need this exact help. Without God's initiative ("I will write it on their hearts," Jer. 31:33) you would never make the connection. The Spirit chose to rewrite your inner script, pouring God's love into your heart, inviting you to live in a new reality. He awakens your sense of need, gives you ears to hear, and freely gives necessary wisdom. Application is a gift, because wisdom is a gift.

Fourth, the application of beloved passages is usually quite straightforward. God states something in general terms. You insert your relevant particulars. For example:

> "Even though I walk through the valley of the shadow of death, I will fear no evil, for you are with me" (Ps. 23:4). What troubles are you facing? Who is with you?

> "All we like sheep have gone astray; we have turned—every one—to his own way; and the LORD has laid on him the iniquity of us all" (Isa. 53:6). What is your particular way of straying? How does the Lamb of God connect with your situation?

"Do not be anxious about anything, but in everything by prayer and supplication with thanksgiving let your requests be made known to God" (Phil. 4:6). With what are you obsessed? What promises anchor your plea for help (Phil. 4:5, 7–9)?

Such words speak to common human experiences. A passage becomes personal when your details participate in what is said. The gap across centuries and between cultures seems almost to disappear. Your God is a very present help in trouble—this trouble. Application occurs in specifics.

2. LOOK FOR THE DIRECTLY APPLICABLE PASSAGES

How do you widen your scope of application? Keep your eye out for *straightforward passages*. Typically they generalize or summarize in some manner, inviting personal appropriation. Consider the core promises of God, the joys and sorrows of many psalms, the moral divide in many proverbs, the call of many commands, the summary comment that interprets a story. As examples of the first, Exodus 34:6–7; Numbers 6:24–26; and Deuteronomy 31:6 state foundational promises that are repeatedly and variously applied throughout the rest of Scripture. Pay attention to how subsequent scriptures specifically reapply these statements, and to how the entire Bible illustrates them. Make such promises part of your repertoire of well-pondered truth. They are important for a reason. Get a feel for how these words come to a point in Jesus Christ and can rescript every life, including yours.

Consider how *generalization* occurs. In narratives, details make the story come to life. But psalms and proverbs adopt the opposite strategy. They intentionally flatten out specific references, so anyone can identify. David was troubled when he wrote Psalm 25—his emotions are clearly felt. But he left his own story at the door: "For your name's sake, O Lord, pardon my guilt, for it is great. . . . Consider my affliction and my trouble, and forgive all my sins" (Ps. 25:11, 18). He gives no details. We are given a template flexible enough to embrace any one of us. As you reapply, *your* sins and sufferings make Psalm 25 come to life as it leads you to mercy.

In matters of obedience, the Bible often proclaims a general truth without mentioning any of the multitude of possible applications. When Jesus says, "You cannot serve God and money" (Luke 16:13), he leaves you to puzzle out the forms of money-worship particular to your personality and your culture. In such cases, the Bible speaks in large categories, addressing many different experiences, circumstances, and actions. Sorting out what it specifically means is far from being mechanical and automatic, but the application process follows a rather direct line.

If you have a favorite Bible passage, it is likely one of these parts of Scripture whose application is relatively direct. But our experience of immediate relevance can skew our expectations for how the rest of God's revelation applies to our lives.

3. RECOGNIZE THE SORTS OF PASSAGES WHERE PERSONAL APPLICATION IS LESS DIRECT

Here is the core dilemma. Most of the Bible does *not* speak directly and personally to you. How do you "apply" the stories in Genesis? What about genealogies and census data? Leviticus? The life stories of Esther, Job, Samson, or Paul? The distribution of land and villages in Joshua? The history of Israel's decline detailed through 1 and 2 Kings? The prophetic woes scorching Moab, Philistia, Egypt, and Babylon, fulfilled so long ago? The ruminations of Ecclesiastes? The Gospel stories showing Jesus in action? The New Testament's frequent preoccupation with Jew-Gentile relations? The apocalyptic images in the Revelation?

The Bible's stories, histories, and prophecies—even many of the commands, teachings, promises, and prayers—take thoughtful work in order to reapply with current relevance. If you receive them directly—as if they speak directly to you, about you, with your issues in view—you will misunderstand and misapply Scripture. For example, the angel's command to Joseph, "take the child and his mother, and flee to Egypt" (Matt. 2:13), is not a command to anyone today to buy a ticket to Egypt! Those who attempt to take the entire Bible as if it directly applies today end up distorting the Bible. It becomes an omnirelevant magic book teeming with private messages and meanings. God does not intend that his words function that way.

These passages *do* apply. But most of the Bible applies differently from the passages tilted toward immediate relevance. What you read applies by extension and analogy, not directly. Less sizzle, but quietly significant. In one sense, such passages apply exactly because they are *not* about you. Understood rightly, such passages give a changed perspective. They locate you on a bigger stage. They teach you to notice God and other people in their own right. They call you to understand yourself within a story—many stories—bigger than your personal history and immediate concerns. They locate you within a community far wider than your immediate network of relationships. And they remind you that you are always in God's presence, under his eye, and part of his program.

4. TACKLE THE APPLICATION OF LESS-DIRECT PASSAGES

Application is a lifelong process, seeking to expand and deepen wisdom. At the simplest level, simply read through the Bible in its larger chunks. The cumulative acquisition of wisdom is hard to quantify. A sense of what truth means and how truth works is overheard as well as heard. But also wrestle to work out the implications of specific passages.

Consider two examples. The first presents an extreme challenge to personal application: a genealogy or census. These are directly *irrelevant* to your life. Your name is not on the list. The reasons for the list disappeared long ago. You gain nothing by knowing that "Koz fathered Anub, Zobebah, and the clans of Aharhel" (1 Chron. 4:8). But when you learn to listen rightly, such lists intend many good things—and each list has a somewhat different purpose. Among the things taught are these:

- The Lord writes down names in his book of life.
- Families and communities matter to him.
- God is faithful to his promises through long history.
- He enlists his people as troops in the redemptive reconquest of a world gone bad.
- All the promises of God find their "Yes" in Jesus Christ (2 Cor. 1:20).

You "apply" a list of ancient names and numbers by extension, not directly. Your love for God grows surer and more intelligent when you ponder the *kind* of thing this is, rather than getting lost in the blizzard of names or numbers.

The second example presents a midlevel challenge. Psalms are often among the most directly relevant parts of Scripture. But what do you do when Psalm 21:1 says, "O LORD, in your strength the king rejoices"? The psalm is not talking about you, and it is not you talking—not directly. A train of connected truths apply this psalm to you, leading you out of yourself.

First, David lived and wrote these words, but Jesus Christ most fully lived—is now living, and will finally fulfill—this entire psalm. He is the greatest human king singing this song of deliverance; and he is also the divine Lord whose power delivers. We know from the perspective of New Testament fulfillment that this psalm is overtly by and about Jesus, not about any particular individual.

Second, you participate in the triumph of your King. You are caught up in all that the psalm describes, because you are in this Christ. So pay attention to *his* experience, because he includes you.

Third, your participation arises not as a solo individual but in company with countless brothers and sisters. You most directly apply this psalm by joining with fellow believers in a chorus of heartfelt gladness: "O Lord . . . *we* will sing and praise your power" (Ps. 21:13). The king's opening joy in God's power has become his people's closing joy.

Finally, figuratively, you are also kingly in Christ. In this sense, Jesus's experience of deliverance (the entire psalm) does apply to your life. Having walked through the psalm as an expression of the exultant triumph of Christ Jesus himself, you may now make it your experience too. You could even adapt Psalm 21 into the first person, inserting "I/me/my" in place of "the king" and "he/him/his." It would be blasphemous to do that at first. It is fully proper and your exceeding joy to do this in the end. This is a song in which all heaven will join. As you grasp that your brothers and sisters share this same goal, you will love them and serve their joy more consistently.

God reveals himself and his purposes throughout Scripture. Wise application always starts there.

CONCLUSION

You started by identifying one passage that speaks persistently, directly, and relevantly into your life. You have seen how both the direct and the indirect passages intend to change you. Learning to wisely apply the harder, less relevant passages has a surprising benefit. Your whole Bible "applies personally." This Lord is your God; this history is your history; these people are your people;

this Savior has brought you in to participate in who he is and what he does. Venture out into the remotest regions of Scripture, seeking to know and love your God better.

Hopefully, you better understand why your most reliable passage so changed your life. Ponder those familiar words once more. You will notice that they also lift you out of self-preoccupation, out of the double evil of sin and misery. God brought his gracious care to you through that passage and rearranged your life. You love him who first loved you, so you love his other children. And that is how the whole Bible, and each of its parts, applies personally.

7

READING THE BIBLE FOR PREACHING AND PUBLIC WORSHIP

R. Kent Hughes

The Bible, as holy Scripture, is the only certain source of God's words in the entire world. Paul's statement that "All Scripture is breathed out by God" (2 Tim. 3:16) means that all the words of the Bible are God's words to us. Therefore if we want to hear our Creator and Lord speaking to us, we must continually give attention to the authoritative words of the Bible. This means that the Bible must be the only true foundation and constant guide for all that we do in the life of the church, and the Bible must be central to all that happens in preaching and public worship.

Moses and Jesus confirm how God's people are to regard his holy Word. On the very day that Moses completed the writing of the Book of the Law, he directed that it be placed beside the ark (Deut. 31:26), sang his final song (the great Song of Moses; Deut. 31:30–32:43), and then declared that "it is no empty word for you, but your very life" (Deut. 32:47). Moses's declaration set the standard for the primacy and sufficiency of God's Word (see Psalms 19 and 119). A millennium and a half later Jesus, the second Moses, after defeating Satan with three deft quotations from Deuteronomy, declared, "Man shall not live by bread alone, but by every word that comes from the mouth of God" (Matt. 4:4). The Scriptures were life to Moses and food to Jesus; as such they together establish the ideal for God's people and directly inform the Bible's use in preaching and public worship. Jesus's dependence on the sufficiency and potency of God's Word raised the standard high for all apostolic and postapostolic preaching and worship.

THE BIBLE'S USE IN PREACHING

When the apostle Paul instructs his younger colleague Timothy in the conduct of public worship, he places the Bible at its very center: "Until I come, devote yourself to the public reading of Scripture, to exhortation, to teaching. . . . Practice these things, immerse yourself in them" (1 Tim. 4:13, 15). Paul's direction was: read the Word; preach the Word (see 2 Tim. 4:2)! The early church sought to follow Paul's exhortation. Justin Martyr, writing circa AD 150–155, describes a typical Lord's Day: "On the day called Sunday, all who live in cities or in the country gather together in one place, and the memoirs of the apostles and the writings of the prophets are read, as long as time permits; then, when the reader has finished, the president speaks, instructing and exhorting the people to imitate these good things."[1] In other words, the practice of these earliest churches was that the Scripture was to be read, and then preaching was to be based on that reading of the Word.

[1] Justin Martyr, *First Apology*, 1.67.

From the Text

Paul directs Timothy, "Do your best to present yourself to God as one approved, a worker who has no need to be ashamed, rightly handling the word of truth" (2 Tim. 2:15). "Rightly handling" is a compound word in Greek, in which the first part comes from the Greek word *orthos*—"straight." The exact charge to Timothy is to impart the word of truth *without deviation* and *without dilution*—to get it straight and give it straight! The preacher must preach the text, not the idea that brought him to the text. He must stand behind the Bible, not in front of it. He must preach what the passage says, not what he wants it to say.

Good preaching requires prayerfully interpreting the text in its context. This involves using the established rules of interpretation; understanding the text's application both in its historical setting and in the whole of Scripture; discerning how it is a revelation of Jesus Christ and making the appropriate biblical connections; taking the trip from Jerusalem to one's own town and coming to see its present relevance; articulating the theme of the text; using stories and illustrations that truly illuminate the text; and employing language that actually communicates in today's culture.

From the Heart

However, the proper use of the Bible in preaching requires more than good hermeneutics and homiletics; it also requires a heart that has been softened and prepared and sanctified by the Word that is to be preached. The Puritan William Ames (1576–1633) expressed it well:

> Next to the evidence of truth, and the will of God drawn out of the Scriptures, nothing makes a sermon more to pierce, than when it comes out of the inward affection of the heart without any affectation. To this purpose it is very profitable, if besides the daily practice of piety we use serious meditation

and fervent prayer to work those things upon our own hearts, which we would persuade others of.[2]

Every appropriation of the truth preached will strengthen the preacher for preaching. Every act of repentance occasioned in his soul by the Word he now preaches will give conviction to his voice.

Jonathan Edwards's *Treatise Concerning the Religious Affections* has provided the best explanation of what must take place within the preacher. By "affections" Edwards meant one's *heart*, one's *inclinations*, and one's *will*. As Edwards said, "true religion *consists in a great measure* in vigorous and lively actings and the inclination and will of the soul, or the fervent exercises of the heart." Edwards demonstrates from a cascade of Scriptures that real Christianity so impacts the affections that it shapes one's fears, hopes, loves, hatreds, desires, joys, sorrows, gratitudes, compassions, and zeals.

This is what should routinely happen to the preacher: the message should work its way through his whole intellectual and moral being as he prepares for and practices the proclamation of God's Word. When the message has affected him deeply, then he is ready to preach. Sermon preparation is twenty hours of prayer. It is humble, holy, critical thinking. It is repeatedly asking the Holy Spirit for insight. It is the word penetrating into the depths of the preacher's own soul. It is ongoing repentance. It is utter dependence. It is a singing heart.

THE BIBLE'S USE IN PUBLIC WORSHIP

God's Word deserves great reverence from his people. Isaiah writes, "But this is the one to whom I will look: he who is humble and contrite in spirit and trembles at my word" (Isa. 66:2). Therefore when Scripture is read aloud in a worship service,

[2] Quoted in Art Lindsley, "Profiles in Faith, William Ames: Practical Theologian," *Tabletalk* 7/3 (June 1983): 14.

the reader and the congregation should take care to convey the reverent attention that Scripture deserves.

From its earliest days the church gave primacy to the reading of Holy Scripture, as seen in the apostle Paul's aforementioned charge to Timothy to devote himself to "the public reading of Scripture," as well as Justin Martyr's account of the apostolic church's practice of reading "the memoirs of the apostles and writings of the prophets . . . as long as time permits." The regular custom soon was to have two extended public readings, one from the Old Testament and one from the New Testament.

Reading of Scripture

Every Bible-believing church must give preeminence to Scripture in its public services of worship. This means that the Scripture to be expounded should be read aloud, and should be set forth in its full context. After all, the reading of God's Word is the one place where we can be sure that we are hearing God. Responsive readings can be beneficial because they involve the congregation in voicing the sacred text.

There is substantial wisdom in keeping to the apostolic church's custom of reading passages from the Old Testament and New Testament in pairs, as it were, because this practice weekly reaffirms the continuity of the two Testaments, encourages biblical theology, and counters the tendencies of many today to pit the two Testaments against each other. It also substantially contributes to the service as a service of the Word in its unity and fullness.

Congregational response to the reading with a hearty "Amen!" or the time-honored "Thanks be to God" can further elevate the corporate assent to the centrality and authority of God's Word. Jerome said of the congregational "Amen" in his day that at times it "seemed like a crack of thunder." How glorious and how good for the soul!

Of course, such attention to God's Word can also prove ineffective if the reading itself is left to a last-minute assignment, such that the reader fails to prepare mentally and spiritually for what he or she is required to do. All of us have heard the Scripture abused by a reader who hasn't the faintest idea of the meaning of what he is reading, or by reading too fast, or mispronouncing common words, or by losing his place. This is not to suggest that the Scripture is to be read as dramatically as possible or performed as a reader's theater. But how God-honoring it is to read God's Word well, with a prayerful spirit. Pastors and readers can serve their congregations well by prayerfully reading the text a dozen times with pencil in hand *before* reading it to God's people.

A Service of the Word

The Bible's use in preaching and public worship should be in such a way as to result in a Christ-exalting service of the Word. This requires work by the preacher and the leaders of the congregation, so that God's Word is read to his glory, the sermon is derived from the faithful exposition of the text reading, and the reading and preaching of the biblical passage is set in the context of songs and hymns and programs that are redolent with the substance of God's holy Word.

Part 3

THE CANON
OF SCRIPTURE

8

THE CANON
OF THE OLD TESTAMENT

Roger T. Beckwith

The word "canon" (Gk. for "a rule") is applied to the Bible in two ways: first, in regard to the Bible as the church's *standard* of faith and practice, and second, in regard to its contents as the *correct collection and list* of inspired books. The word was first applied to the identity of the biblical books in the latter part of the fourth century AD, reflecting the fact that there had recently been a need to settle some Christians' doubts on the matter. Before this, Christians had referred to the "Old Testament" and "New Testament" as the "Holy Scriptures" and had assumed, rather than made explicit, that they were the *correct* collections and lists.

THE CAUSES OF UNCERTAINTY ABOUT
THE OLD TESTAMENT CANON

The Christian Old Testament corresponded to the Hebrew Bible, which Jesus and the first Christians inherited from the Jews. In

71

the Gentile mission of the church, however, it was necessary to use the Septuagint (a translation of the Old Testament that had been made in pre-Christian times for Greek-speaking Alexandrian Jews). Because knowledge of Hebrew was uncommon in the church (especially outside Syria and Palestine), the first Latin translation of the Old Testament came from the Septuagint and not from the original Hebrew. Where there was no knowledge of Hebrew and little acquaintance with Jewish tradition, it became harder to distinguish between the biblical books and other popular religious reading matter circulating in the Greek or Latin language. These factors led to the uncertainty about the composition of Scripture, which the coiners of the term "canon" sought to settle.

DID THE HEBREW BIBLE CONTAIN THE SAME BOOKS AS TODAY'S OLD TESTAMENT?

The above analysis assumes that the Hebrew Bible, which the church inherited in the first century, comprised the same books as it does today, and that uncertainty developed only later. Many in modern times have denied this view, but for mistaken reasons.

Are the Sections of Scripture Arbitrary Groups, Canonized in Different Eras?

Until recently, the accepted critical view was that the three sections of the Hebrew Bible—the Law, the Prophets, and the Writings (or Hagiographa)—were arbitrary groupings of books acknowledged as canonical in three different eras: the first section in the time of Ezra and Nehemiah (fifth century BC); the last section at the synod of Jabneh or Jamnia (as late as AD 90); and the middle section sometime in between (perhaps in the third century BC). The reasons given for the datings were as follows: (1) Because the Samaritans acknowledged only the Pentateuch (the five books of the Law) as Scripture, therefore the Pentateuch must have constituted the whole Jewish canon when the Samaritan schism took place at the time of Ezra and Nehemiah. (2) Because the synod of Jamnia discussed the canonicity of Ecclesiastes, the Song of Solomon, and presumably the other three books with which some rabbis had problems (Ezekiel, Proverbs, and Esther), these must still have been outside the Canon at the time. (3) Chronicles and Daniel, which are found in the Writings section of the Hebrew Bible, would have belonged more naturally with Kings and the oracular Prophets than with the Hagiographa; from this it was concluded that the Prophets section had been closed too soon to include them.

Recent study, however, has demolished this hypothesis. The five books of the Law are obviously not an arbitrary grouping. They follow a chronological sequence, concentrate on the Law of Moses, and trace history from the creation of the world to Moses's death. Moreover, the Prophets and the Writings, if arranged in the traditional order recorded in the Talmud (see fig. 8.1), are not arbitrary groupings either. The Prophets begin with four narrative books—Joshua, Judges, Samuel, and Kings—tracing history through a second period, from the entry into the Promised Land to the Babylonian exile. They end with four oracular books—Jeremiah, Ezekiel, Isaiah, and the Book of the Twelve (Minor Prophets)—arranged in descending order of size. The Hagiographa (Writings) begin with six lyrical or wisdom books—Psalms, Job, Proverbs, Ecclesiastes, Song of Solomon, and Lamentations—arranged in descending order of size, and end with four narrative books—Daniel, Esther, Ezra–Nehemiah, and Chronicles—covering a third period of history, the period of the exile and the return. (The remaining book of the Writings, Ruth, is prefixed to Psalms, since it ends with the genealogy of the psalmist David.) The four narrative books in the Hagiographa are this time put second, so that Chronicles can sum up the whole biblical story, from Adam to the return from exile, and for this reason also Ezra–Nehemiah is put before Chronicles, not after it. A small anomaly is that the Song of Solomon is in fact slightly shorter than Lamentations, not longer, but it is put first to keep the three books related to Solomon together. That Daniel is treated as a narrative book may be surprising, but it is undeniable that it begins with six chapters of narrative.

Each of the three sections of the Old Testament canon has a *narrative component*, covering one of three successive periods of history, and a *literary component*, representing one of three different types of religious literature: law, oracles, and lyrics or wisdom. The narrative material is, as far as possible, arranged in chronological order, and the literary material, when not united with the narrative material (as in the Pentateuch), is arranged in descending order of size. The shape of the Canon is therefore no accident of history but a work of art, and in its final form must be due to a single thinker, living before circa 130 BC, when the three sections are first mentioned in the Greek prologue to *Sirach* (in the Apocrypha).

The datings assigned to the recognition of the three sections are also misconceived. First, it is now known that the Samaritans continued to follow Jewish customs long after the time of Ezra and Nehemiah, and that the schism did not become complete until the Jews destroyed the Samaritan temple on Mount Gerizim in about 110 BC. It seems that the Samaritans only then rejected the Prophets and Writings because of the recognition those books give to the temple at Jerusalem.

Second, the problems that some rabbis had with as many as five biblical books do not mean that those books were outside the Canon, since the rabbinical literature notes similar problems with many other biblical books, including all five books of the Pentateuch. The problems with the five disputed books may have been particularly difficult, but they, too, were eventually solved in the same way as the other problems. There was no "synod of

Jamnia," but simply a discussion at its academy that confirmed the canonicity of Ecclesiastes and the Song of Solomon—though that discussion did not end the controversy. Esther, in particular, continued to be discussed long after AD 90. Further, the same kinds of questions were raised about Ezekiel, which is found in the Prophets, not in the Writings; if the reasoning of the critical view were sound, then the Prophets also could not have been in the Canon, which would be absurd.

Third, contrary to what the critical view suggested, there would have been no strong incentive to put Chronicles and Daniel in the Prophets, since they were both being treated as narrative books relating to the final period of Old Testament history and therefore belonging in the Hagiographa.

Fig. 8.1 The Traditional Order of Old Testament Canonical Books according to the Talmud

The Law
Chronological (from the creation of the world to Moses's death): Genesis, Exodus, Leviticus, Numbers, Deuteronomy
The Prophets
Narrative books (from the entry into the Promised Land to the Babylonian exile): Joshua, Judges, Samuel, Kings
Oracular books (in descending order of size): Jeremiah, Ezekiel, Isaiah, The Book of the Twelve
The Writings
Lyrical/wisdom books (in descending order of size): Psalms (with Ruth prefixed), Job, Proverbs, Ecclesiastes, Song of Songs, Lamentations
Narrative books (from the period of exile to the return): Daniel, Esther, Ezra–Nehemiah, Chronicles

Was There a Distinct Alexandrian Canon?

A further fallacious argument that many critics have used to show that the Old Testament canon was still open at the beginning of the Christian era is the hypothesis of a distinct Alexandrian canon, including at least some of the apocryphal books. For discussion of this argument, see "How the Greek and Latin Translations Came to Contain the Apocrypha" on pages 91–92.

Did the Qumran Sect Have a Broader Old Testament Canon?

The discovery of the Dead Sea Scrolls at Qumran has turned the attention of critics to the pseudepigrapha—notably *1 Enoch*, *The Testament of Levi*, *Jubilees*, and *The Temple Scroll*. It is today frequently claimed that the men of Qumran (probably Essenes) had a broad canon that included these books. But it should be noted that (1) the pseudonyms used in these works belong to the biblical period, indicating a recognition that prophetic inspiration had now ceased; (2) the inspiration claimed at Qumran was an inspiration to *interpret* the Scriptures, not to add to them; (3) the quotations from authoritative works made in the Qumran writings are almost exclusively from the Old Testament books, and the formulas used for quoting Scripture are not used with the few quotations from elsewhere; and (4) though the Essenes may have added an interpretative appendix to the three standard sections of the Old Testament canon, containing their favored pseudepigrapha, it is significant that they did not try to insert them into the three standard sections, which were now evidently closed (i.e., seen as complete).

THE TRUTH ABOUT THE OLD TESTAMENT CANON

So much for fashionable errors regarding the assembling and recognition of the Old Testament canon. The true evidence of the process is comparatively simple. First, it was recognized from ancient times that, if revelation was to be preserved, it needed to be written down (see Ex. 17:14; Deut. 31:24–26; Ps. 102:18; Isa. 30:8). This process of writing the words had been begun by God himself at Mount Sinai, when he gave Moses the two tablets of stone with his own words written on them: "The tablets were the work of God, and the writing was the writing of God, engraved on the tablets" (Ex. 32:16). These tablets were deposited in the ark of the covenant (Deut. 10:5), and were the basis of the covenant relationship between God and his people. Then, later writings were added to "the Book of the Covenant" (see Ex. 24:7; Josh. 24:26; 2 Kings 23:2). A significant object lesson on the importance of preserving God's words in written form was the later discovery of the Book of the Law by Hilkiah, after it had been lost during the reigns of Manasseh and Amon: its teaching came as a great shock because it had been forgotten (2 Kings 22–23; 2 Chronicles 34).

Second, on great national occasions the Book of the Law was read to the people (Ex. 24:7; 2 Kings 23:2; Neh. 8:9, 14–17; etc.). Deuteronomy provides for it to be read regularly every seven years (Deut. 31:10–13). An extension of the same practice was the later reading of the Pentateuch in the synagogue on the Sabbath, supplemented by a reading from the Prophets (Luke 4:16–20; Acts 13:15, 27; 15:21; etc.).

Third, Deuteronomy was to be laid up in the sanctuary (Deut. 31:24–26), and that was where Hilkiah found the Book of the Law (2 Kings 22:8; 2 Chron. 34:15). It is known from Josephus and the earliest rabbinical literature that the practice of laying up the Scriptures in the temple still continued down to the first century AD. To lay up any book there as Scripture must have been a solemn and carefully deliberated act of national significance.

Fourth, the calendar of the book of *1 Enoch*, followed at Qumran, seems to have been devised in about the third century BC so as to avoid having any dated act recorded in the Scriptures occur on the Sabbath. At least ten (and probably more) of the present Old Testament books are shown to be acknowledged as canonical at this time by this listing.

Fifth, *Sirach* 44–49, written about 180 BC, provides a catalog of famous men, and these are probably all meant to be biblical figures, since they are all now found in the Bible. The end of *Sirach* 49 sums them up, while chapter 50 moves on to describe Simon the son of Onias, a later worthy figure not found in the Bible. Accounting for these men raises the number of books to at least sixteen for which there is specific extrabiblical attestation to canonicity.

Sixth, Josephus relates that the Pharisees, Sadducees, and Essenes first became distinct and rival schools of thought in the time of Jonathan Maccabeus (d. 143 BC). To alter the Canon after this time would have been very controversial, and can hardly have occurred. So the Canon must have been acknowledged as closed before 143 BC.

Seventh, the final touches may have been put to the Canon in 165 BC by Judas Maccabeus (making it a listed collection of twenty-four books in three sections, beginning with Genesis and ending with Chronicles; see fig. 8.1), when he gathered the scattered Scriptures after Antiochus's persecution (2 Macc. 2:14). This is the Bible that, two centuries later, the New Testament and other first-century writings reflect.

Eighth, in spite of numerous differences between Jesus and the Jewish religious leaders of his time, there is no record of any dispute between them, or any later dispute with Jesus's apostles, over which Old Testament books were canonical. The Old Testament canon accepted by the early church was identical to the canon of books accepted by the Jewish people.

Ninth, Jesus and the New Testament authors quote the words of the Old Testament approximately three hundred times (see fig. 19.1; uncertainty about the exact number arises because of a few instances where it is not clear whether it is an Old Testament quotation or only an echoing expression using similar words). They regularly quote it as having divine authority, with phrases such as "it is written," "Scripture says," and "God says," but no other writings are quoted in this way. Occasionally the New Testament writers will quote some other authors, even pagan Greek authors (see Acts 17:28; Titus 1:12–13; Jude 8–10, 14–16), but they never quote these other sources as being the words of God, as they do the canonical Old Testament books.

Tenth, Josephus (born AD 37/38) explained, "From Artaxerxes to our own times a complete history has been written, but has not been deemed worthy of equal credit with the earlier record, because of the failure of the exact succession of the prophets."[1] Josephus was aware of the writings now considered part of the Apocrypha, but he (and, he implies, mainstream Jewish opinion) considered these other writings "not . . . worthy of equal credit" with what are now known as the Old Testament Scriptures.

Eleventh, additional Jewish tradition after the time of the New Testament also expresses the conviction that no more prophetic writings had been given after the time of the last Old Testament prophets Haggai, Zechariah, and Malachi.[2]

Sound historical study shows, therefore, that the Hebrew Old Testament contains the true canon of the Old Testament, shared by Jesus and the apostles with first-century Judaism. No books are left out that should be included, and none are included that should be left out.

[1] Josephus, *Against Apion*, 1.41.
[2] See Babylonian Talmud, *Yoma* 9b; *Sotah* 48b; *Sanhedrin* 11a; and *Midrash Rabbah on Song of Songs* 8.9.3.

9

THE CANON
OF THE NEW TESTAMENT

Charles E. Hill

The foundations for a New Testament canon lie not, as some
would assert, in the needs or the practices of the church in the
second, third, and fourth centuries AD, but in the gracious purpose
of a self-revealing God whose word carries his own divine authority.
Just as new outpourings of divine word-revelation accompanied
and followed each major act of redemption in the ancient history
of God's people (the covenant with Adam and Eve, the covenant
with Abraham, the redemption from Egypt, the establishment of
the monarchy, the exile, and the restoration), so when the promised
Messiah came, a new and generous outpouring of divine revelation
necessarily ensued (see 2 Tim. 1:8–11; Titus 1:1–3).

THE OLD TESTAMENT AUTHORIZATION
The prospect of a New Testament Scripture to stand alongside
the Old Testament was anticipated, even authorized, in the Old

Testament itself, embedded in the promise of God's ultimate act of redemption through the Messiah, in faithfulness to his covenant (Jer. 31:31–33; cf. Heb. 8:7–13; 10:16–18). Jesus taught his disciples after his resurrection that "the Law of Moses and the Prophets and the Psalms" predicted not only the Messiah's suffering and resurrection but also that "repentance and forgiveness of sins should be proclaimed in his name to all nations, beginning from Jerusalem" (Luke 24:44–48). Prophetic passages such as Isaiah 2:2–3; 49:6; and Psalm 2:8 spoke of a time when the light of God's grace in redemption would be proclaimed to all nations. It naturally follows that this proclamation would eventuate in a new collection of written Scriptures complementing the books of the old covenant—both from the pattern of God's redemptive work in the past (mentioned above) and from the actual writing ministry of some of Jesus's apostles (and their associates) in the accomplishment of their commission.

THE COMMISSION OF JESUS

God, who spoke in many and various ways in times past, chose to speak in these last days to mankind through his Son (see Heb. 1:1–2, 4). Bringing this saving message to Israel and the nations was a crucial part of the mission of Jesus Christ (Isa. 49:6; Acts 26:23), the Word made flesh (John 1:14). He put this mission into effect through chosen apostles, whom he commissioned to be his authoritative representatives ("whoever receives you receives me," Matt. 10:40). Their assignment was to "bring to . . . remembrance," through the work of the Spirit, his words and works (John 14:26; 16:13–14) and to bear witness to Jesus "in Jerusalem and in all Judea and Samaria, and to the end of the earth" (Acts 1:8; see Matt. 28:19–20; Luke 24:47–48; John 17:14, 20). In time, the apostolic preaching came to written form in the books of the New Testament, which now function as "the commandment of the Lord and Savior through your apostles" (2 Pet. 3:2).

Paul and the other apostles wrote just as they preached: conscious of Jesus's mandate. From the beginning, the full authority of the apostles (and prophets) to deliver God's word was recognized, at least by many (Acts 10:22; Eph. 2:20; 1 Thess. 2:13; Jude 17–18). This recognition is accordingly reflected in the earliest nonapostolic writers. For example, Clement of Rome attested that "the apostles received the gospel for us from the Lord Jesus Christ; Jesus the Christ was sent forth from God. So then Christ is from God, and the apostles are from Christ. Both, therefore, came of the will of God in good order."[1]

THE RECOGNITION OF NEW COVENANT SCRIPTURES

As God's word to mankind, the "God-breathed" Scripture (2 Tim. 3:16) is self-attesting, and thus the Canon may be said to be self-establishing. Yet history records that for centuries there were variations in local church practice and disagreements among churches and early theologians about several books of the New Testament. Such variations, however, are not unexpected, given that the process of recognition involved more than two dozen books that came into being over a period of perhaps fifty years, circulating unsystematically to churches as they were springing up in widely diffused parts of the Roman Empire.

In its deliberations about the particular books that make up the canon of Scripture, the church did not sovereignly "determine" or "choose" the books it most preferred—whether for catechetical, polemical, liturgical, or edificatory purposes. Rather, the church saw itself as empowered only to receive and recognize what God had provided in books handed down from the apostles

---

[1] Clement of Rome, *1 Clement* 42.1–2, written c. AD 95.

and their immediate companions.[2] This is why discussions of the so-called "criteria" of canonicity can be misleading. Qualities such as "apostolicity," "antiquity," "orthodoxy," "liturgical use," and "church consensus" are not criteria by which the church autonomously judged which documents it would receive. The first three are qualities the church recognizes in the voice of its Savior, to which voice the church willingly submits itself ("My sheep hear my voice . . . and they follow me," John 10:27).

The Gospels according to Matthew, Mark, Luke, and John (the earliest Gospels known) gained universal acceptance while arousing very little controversy within the church. If the latest of these, the Gospel of John, was published near the end of the first century (as most scholars think), it is remarkable that its words are echoed around AD 110 in the writings of Ignatius of Antioch, who also knew Matthew, and perhaps Luke. At about the same time, Papias of Hierapolis in Asia Minor received traditions about the origins of Matthew's and Mark's Gospels, and quite probably Luke's and John's. In the middle of the second century, Justin Martyr in Rome reported that the Gospels (apparently the four)—which he calls "memoirs of the apostles"—were being read and exposited in Christian services of worship.

In 2 Peter 3:16, a collection of at least some of Paul's letters was already known and regarded as Scripture and therefore enjoyed canonical endorsement. Furthermore, a collection (of unknown extent) of Paul's letters was known to Clement of Rome and to the recipients of his letter in Corinth before the end of the first century, then also to Ignatius of Antioch and Polycarp of Smyrna and their readers in the early second century. The Pastoral Letters (1–2 Timothy and Titus), rejected as Paul's by many modern critics, are attested at least from the time of Polycarp.

By the end of the second century a "core" collection of New Testament books—twenty-one of the twenty-seven—was gen-

[2] For example, Iranaeus, *Against Heresies*, 3.1.1–2.

erally recognized: four Gospels, Acts, thirteen epistles of Paul, 1 Peter, 1 John, and Revelation. By this time Hebrews (accepted in the East and by Irenaeus and Tertullian in the West, but questioned in Rome due to doubts about authorship), James, 2 Peter, 2 and 3 John, and Jude were only minimally attested in the writings of church leaders. This infrequent citation led to the expression of doubts by later fathers.[3] Yet, by some time in the third century, codices (precursors of the modern book form, as opposed to scrolls) containing all seven of the "general epistles" were being produced, and Eusebius reports that all seven were "known to most."

An unusual case is the book of Revelation, which seems to have been accepted everywhere at first (in the West by Justin, Irenaeus, the Muratorian Fragment, and Tertullian; in the East by Clement of Alexandria and Origen). But due to its exploitation by Montanists and others, it was criticized by Gaius, a Roman writer in the early third century. Several decades later, Dionysius of Alexandria, while not rejecting the book, argued that it could not have been written by the apostle John. These factors led to enduring doubts in the East and to Revelation's absence from later Eastern canon lists, though its reputation in the West did not suffer.

To complicate matters, many documents were produced in the course of the second century that in some way paralleled or imitated New Testament books. Many of these made some claim to apostolic authority, and some gained considerable popularity in certain quarters. One or more "Gospels" written in Aramaic attracted interest because of a presumed connection to an original Aramaic Matthew. Other "Gospels" were essentially combinations of the four (i.e., *The Gospel of Peter* and *The Egerton Gospel*), a practice that culminated in Tatian's *Diatessaron*, a

[3] For example, Eusebius, *Ecclesiastical History*, 2.23.25.

harmony of the four (c. AD 172), which was the first form of the Gospels translated into Syriac.

There was a profusion of "Acts" literature, usually following, in novel-like fashion, the fictional exploits of a single apostle (Paul, John, Andrew, Peter). Letters forged in the name of Paul (*To the Laodiceans*, *To the Alexandrians*, *3 Corinthians*) sought to attract adherents to an assortment of special causes. Works in various genres written to advance unorthodox interpretations of Christianity often borrowed the names of apostles (*Apocryphon of John*, *Gospel of Thomas*). In addition, a few writings, probably never intended to be regarded as Scripture, were honored as such by some Christians partly because of assumed authorship by companions of apostles (*1* and *2 Clement*, *The Letter of Barnabas*, *The Shepherd of Hermas*).

By the AD 240s Origen (residing in Caesarea in Palestine) acknowledged all twenty-seven of the New Testament books but reported that James, 2 Peter, 2 and 3 John, and Jude were disputed. The situation is virtually the same for Eusebius, writing about sixty years later, who also reports the doubts some had about Hebrews and Revelation. Still, his two categories of "undisputed" and "disputed but known to most" contain only the twenty-seven and no more. He named five other books (*The Acts of Paul*, *The Shepherd of Hermas*, *The Apocalypse of Peter*, *The Letter of Barnabas*, and *The Didache*) which were known to many churches but which, he believed, had to be judged as spurious.

In the year AD 367 the Alexandrian bishop Athanasius, in his annual Easter letter, gave a list of the New Testament books which comprised, with no reservations, all twenty-seven, while naming several others as useful for catechizing but not as scriptural. Several other fourth-century lists essentially concurred, though with various individual deviations outside of the most basic core (four Gospels, Acts, 13 epistles of Paul, 1 Peter, 1 John). Three African synods—at Hippo Regius in AD 393 and at Carthage in 397 and 419—and the influential African bishop Augustine affirmed the twenty-seven–book Canon. It was enshrined in Jerome's Latin translation, the Vulgate, which became the normative Bible for the Western church. In Eastern churches, recognition of Revelation lagged for quite some time. The churches of Syria did not accept Revelation, 2 Peter, 2 and 3 John, or Jude until the fifth (Western Syria) or sixth (Eastern Syria) centuries.

The apostolic word gave birth to the church (Rom. 1:15–17; 10:14–15; James 1:18; 1 Pet. 1:23–25), and the written form of this word remains as the permanent, documentary expression of God's new covenant. It may be said that only the twenty-seven books of the New Testament manifest themselves as belonging to that original, foundational, apostolic witness. They have demonstrated themselves to be the Word of God to the universal church throughout the generations. Here are the pastures to which Christ's sheep from many folds continually come to hear their Shepherd's voice and to follow him.

10

THE APOCRYPHA

Roger T. Beckwith

Larger editions of the English Bible—from the Great Bible of Tyndale and Coverdale (1539) onward—have often included a separate section between the Old Testament and the New Testament titled "The Apocrypha," consisting of additional books and substantial parts of books. The Latin Vulgate Bible translated by Jerome (begun AD 382, completed 405) had placed them in the Old Testament itself—some as separate items and some as attached to or included in the biblical books of Esther, Jeremiah, and Daniel. In Roman Catholic translations of the Bible, such as the Douay Version and the Jerusalem Bible, these items are still placed in their pre-Reformation positions. In Protestant translations, however, the Apocrypha is either omitted altogether or grouped in a separate section.

HOW JEROME'S VULGATE CAME TO CONTAIN THE APOCRYPHA

In distinguishing the Apocrypha from the Old Testament books, the Protestant translators were not doing something completely novel but were carrying out more thoroughly than ever before the principles on which Jerome (AD 345–420) had made his great Latin Vulgate translation of the Old Testament. The Vulgate was translated from the original Hebrew. But a translation prior to the Vulgate, the Old Latin translation, had been made from the Greek Old Testament, the Septuagint (or LXX). At some stage, early or late, additional books and parts of books, which were not in the Hebrew Bible, had found their way into the Greek Old Testament, and from there into the Old Latin version. Jerome retained these in his new translation, the Latin Vulgate, but added prefaces at various points to emphasize that they were not true parts of the Bible, and he called them by the name "apocrypha" (Gk. *apokrypha*, "those having been hidden away"). In accordance with his teaching—and with the understanding of the Old Testament canon held by Jesus, the New Testament authors, and the first-century Jews (see chap. 8)—the sixteenth-century Protestant translators did not consider those writings part of the Old Testament but gathered them together in a separate section, to which they gave Jerome's name, "The Apocrypha."

Jerome's reason for choosing this name is not readily apparent. He probably took a hint from Origen, who a century and a half earlier had stated that the Jews applied this name to the most esteemed of their noncanonical books. Origen and Jerome were two of the most distinguished students of Judaism among the Fathers, so it would be natural for them to use the term in a Jewish sense, though applying it to the noncanonical Jewish books that were most esteemed by Christians. Jews would never destroy respected religious books, but, if unfit for use, such books would be hidden away and left to decay naturally. So "hidden" came to mean "highly esteemed, though uncanonical."

Jerome did not actually confine his name "apocrypha" to Jewish books but used it also of noncanonical Christian books, such as *The Shepherd of Hermas*, which were likewise popular religious reading among Christians. The modern expression "New Testament Apocrypha," for late works that imitate New Testament literature, is similar.

HOW THE GREEK AND LATIN TRANSLATIONS CAME TO CONTAIN THE APOCRYPHA

How the Greek Old Testament, and by consequence the Latin Old Testament, came to contain apocryphal items has been variously understood. Codex Alexandrinus (the great fifth-century AD manuscript of the whole Greek Bible) was printed and published in the eighteenth century. Because it contained the Apocrypha, the editors in the eighteenth century assumed that the Old Testament of this Christian manuscript had been copied from Jewish manuscripts equally inclusive, and that consequently the Apocrypha must have been in the LXX translation, and in the canon of the Greek-speaking Jews of Alexandria who produced it from pre-Christian times (though not in the Bible or canon of the Semitic-speaking Jews of Palestine). This hypothesis held the field for a long time, and a further assumption—that most of the apocryphal books had been composed in Greek, outside Palestine—was made to support it.

All the elements of this theory are now known to be false. (1) Leather manuscripts large enough to contain the whole Old Testament did not exist among either Christians or Jews until the latter part of the fourth century. The earlier Christian biblical manuscripts are on papyrus, and extend only to about three of the larger books. (2) The Jews of Alexandria took their lead largely from Palestine, and would have been unlikely to establish their own distinct canon; moreover, their greatest writer, Philo, though frequently quoting from the Old Testament in his voluminous works, never refers to any of the Apocrypha whatsoever. (3) The earliest Christian biblical manuscripts contain the fewest books of the Apocrypha, and up until AD 313, only *Wisdom, Tobit,* and *Sirach* ever occur in them; other books of the Apocrypha were not added until later. (4) That the Apocrypha was mostly composed in Greek or outside Palestine is no longer widely believed, and *Sirach* (*Ecclesiasticus*) itself states that it was composed in Hebrew (see its prologue; much of its Hebrew text has now been recovered). All the Apocrypha except *Wisdom* and *2 Maccabees* may in fact have been translated from a Hebrew or Aramaic original, written in Palestine.

The way in which Christian writers used the Apocrypha confirms the above analysis. The New Testament seems to reflect knowledge of one or two of the apocryphal texts, but it never ascribes authority to them as it does to many of the canonical Old Testament books. While the New Testament quotes various parts of the Old Testament about three hundred times (see fig. 19.1), it never actually quotes anything from the Apocrypha (Jude 14–16 does not contain a quote from the Apocrypha but from another Jewish writing, *1 Enoch*). In the second century, Justin Martyr and Theophilus of Antioch, who frequently referred to the Old Testament, never referred to any of the Apocrypha. By the end of the second century *Wisdom, Tobit,* and *Sirach* were sometimes being treated as Scripture, but none of the other apocryphal books were. Their eventual acceptance was a slow development. Much the same is true with Christian lists of the Old Testament books: the oldest of them include the fewest of the Apocrypha; and the oldest of all, that of Melito (c. AD 170), includes none.

ACCEPTANCE AND REJECTION
OF THE APOCRYPHA

The growing willingness of the pre-Reformation church to treat the Apocrypha as not just edifying reading but Scripture itself reflected the fact that Christians—especially those living outside Semitic-speaking countries—were losing contact with Jewish tradition. Within those countries, however, a learned Christian tradition akin to elements of Jewish tradition was maintained, especially by scholars such as Origen, Epiphanius, and Jerome, who cultivated the Hebrew language and Jewish studies. By the late fourth century, Jerome found it necessary to assert the distinction between the Apocrypha and the inspired Old Testament books with great emphasis, and a minority of writers continued to make the same distinction throughout the Middle Ages, until the Protestant Reformers arose and made the distinction an important part of their doctrine of Scripture. At the Council of Trent (1545–1563), however, the church of Rome attempted to obliterate the distinction and to put the Apocrypha (with the exception of *1* and *2 Esdras* and *The Prayer of Manasseh*) on the same level as the inspired Old Testament books. This was a consequence of (1) Rome's exalted doctrine of oral tradition, (2) its view that the church creates Scripture, and (3) its acceptance of certain controversial ideas (especially the doctrines of purgatory, indulgences, and works-righteousness as contributing to justification) that were derived from passages in the Apocrypha. These teachings gave support to the Roman Catholic responses to Martin Luther and other leaders of the Protestant Reformation, which had begun in 1517.

Because of these controversial passages, some Protestants ceased to use the Apocrypha altogether. But other Protestants (notably Lutherans and Anglicans), while avoiding such passages and the ideas they contain, continued to read the Apocrypha as generally edifying religious literature. The Apocrypha, together with other postcanonical literature (especially the pseudepigrapha, the Dead Sea Scrolls, the writings of Philo and Josephus, the Targums, and the earliest rabbinical literature) can be helpful in additional ways. They provide the earliest interpretations of the Old Testament literature; they explain what happened in the time between the two Testaments; and they introduce customs, ideas, and expressions that provide a helpful background when reading the New Testament.

THE CONTENTS OF THE APOCRYPHA

Individually, the books of the Apocrypha are fifteen in number (but some count fourteen or twelve by combining some books; see list) and consist of various kinds of literature—narrative, proverbial, prophetic, and liturgical. They probably range in date from the third century BC (*Tobit*) to the first century AD (*2 Esdras* and perhaps *The Prayer of Manasseh*).

1. *First Esdras* (Gk. for "Ezra"), sometimes called *3 Esdras*, covers the same ground as the book of Ezra, with a little of Chronicles and Nehemiah added. It also relates a debate on "the strongest thing in the world."

2. *Second Esdras*, sometimes called *4 Esdras*, is a pseudonymous apocalypse, preserved in Latin, not Greek, with two Christian chapters added at the beginning and two at the end. Chapter 14 gives the number of the Old Testament books. *First* and *Second Esdras* are not included in the Roman Catholic canon.

3. *Tobit* is a moral tale with a Persian background, dealing with almsgiving, marriage, and the burial of the dead.

4. *Judith* is an exciting story, in a confused historical setting, about a pious and patriotic heroine.

5. *The Additions to Esther* are a collection of passages added to the LXX version of Esther, bringing out its religious character.

6. *Wisdom* is a work inspired by Proverbs and written in the person of Solomon.

7. *Sirach*, also called *Ecclesiasticus*, is a work somewhat similar to *Wisdom*, by a named author (Jeshua ben Sira, or Jesus the son of Sirach). It was written about 180 BC, and its catalog of famous men bears important witness to the contents of the Old Testament canon at that date. Its translator's prologue, written half a century later, refers repeatedly to the three sections of the Hebrew Bible. (See chap. 8.)

8. *Baruch* is written in the person of Jeremiah's companion, and somewhat in Jeremiah's manner.

9. *The Epistle of Jeremiah* is connected to *Baruch*, and sometimes the two are counted together as one book (as in the King James Version, which therefore lists fourteen books rather than fifteen).

The Additions to Daniel consist of three segments (10, 11, and 12 in this list):

10. *Susanna* and

11. *Bel and the Dragon* are stories that tell how wise Daniel exposed unjust judges and deceitful pagan priests.

12. *The Song of the Three Young Men* contains a prayer and hymn put into the mouths of Daniel's three companions when they are in the fiery furnace; the hymn is the one used in Christian worship as the *Benedicite* (in the Church of England's services).

As stated before, some authorities count these three books (items 10, 11, and 12) as one book, namely, *The Additions to Daniel*, and they also count *Baruch* as one book that includes *The Epistle of Jeremiah*; in that way, they count only twelve books in the Apocrypha.

13. *The Prayer of Manasseh* puts into words Manasseh's prayer for forgiveness in 2 Chronicles 33:12–13. It is not included in the Roman Catholic canon.

14–15. *First* and *Second Maccabees* relate the successful revolt of the Maccabees against the Hellenistic Syrian persecutor Antiochus Epiphanes in the mid-second century BC. The first book and parts of the second book are the primary historical sources for a knowledge of the Maccabees' heroic faith, though the second book adds legendary material. The LXX also contains a 3 and 4 *Maccabees*, but these are of less importance.

THE DEVELOPMENT OF RELIGIOUS THOUGHT IN THE APOCRYPHA

The development of religious thought found in the Apocrypha, going beyond the teaching of the Old Testament, must be assessed by the teaching of the New Testament. For example, *Wisdom* 4:7–5:16 teaches that all face a personal judgment after this life. This is consistent with later New Testament teaching (Heb. 9:27).

Other teachings add doctrinal material foreign to New Testament teaching, such as the following:

1. In *Tobit* 12:15 seven angels are said to stand before God and present the prayers of the saints.
2. In *2 Maccabees* 15:13–14 a departed prophet is said to pray for God's people on earth.
3. In *Wisdom* 8:19–20 and *Sirach* 1:14 the reader is told that the righteous are those who were given good souls at birth.
4. In *Tobit* 12:9 and *Sirach* 3:3 readers are told that their good deeds atone for their evil deeds.
5. In *2 Maccabees* 12:40–45 the reader is told to pray for the sins of the dead to be forgiven.

The first two ideas find no support in the Old Testament or New Testament, and the second may be thought to give some support to the Roman Catholic idea of prayer to the saints who have died. The last three tenets are clearly at variance with what the New Testament teaches about regeneration, justification, and the present life as one's only period of probation.

The Apocrypha, consequently, must be read with discretion. Though much in it simply reflects Judaism as practiced at a date somewhat later than the Old Testament, and some parts reflect developments in the direction of the New Testament, there are also certain misleading passages that have historical interest but, in terms of Christian theology and practice, are to be avoided.

Part 4

THE RELIABILITY OF BIBLE MANUSCRIPTS

11

THE RELIABILITY
OF THE OLD TESTAMENT
MANUSCRIPTS

Paul D. Wegner

At the beginning of the twentieth century, textual criticism of the Old Testament was in its infancy, with few extant early Hebrew manuscripts. However, with the discoveries of the Dead Sea Scrolls beginning in 1947, scholars found themselves in a better position than ever before to evaluate whether the Old Testament texts are reliable.

At present there exist over three thousand Hebrew manuscripts of the Old Testament, eight thousand manuscripts of the Latin Vulgate, over fifteen hundred manuscripts of the Septuagint, and over sixty-five copies of the Syriac Peshitta.

This article examines the reliability of the Old Testament manuscripts in respect to three main areas: (1) transmission of the Old

Testament; (2) Old Testament textual criticism; and (3) primary Old Testament sources.

TRANSMISSION OF THE OLD TESTAMENT

Jewish tradition maintains that Moses wrote the Pentateuch. If so, then portions of the Old Testament were passed down through scribes for more than three thousand years before becoming part of modern translations. This naturally gives rise to questions like: How did the Old Testament text come about? How were the books copied and by whom? Are the texts available today an accurate reproduction of the originals?

How Did the Old Testament Text Come About?

While some divine revelation may originally have been handed down from generation to generation orally, at some point it was committed to writing to ensure its accuracy. Several biblical passages indicate that from an early period parts of Scripture were held in honor and were considered authoritative (e.g., Ex. 17:14–16; 24:3–4, 7). The stone tablets of the Ten Commandments were to be stored in the ark of the covenant (e.g., Ex. 25:16, 21; Heb. 9:4), and the Book of the Law was to be kept in the tabernacle next to the ark (Deut. 31:24–26). Moses commanded the Israelites to teach God's laws and statutes to their children and grandchildren (Deut. 4:9). The Law of Moses was entrusted to the priests, who were to teach it to the people (Deut. 33:10) and read it aloud publicly every seven years to ensure that the Israelites would remember it (Deut. 31:9–11). They were also commanded not to add to or delete from it at all (Deut. 4:2; 12:32). Both the Old Testament (Josh. 23:6; 1 Kings 2:3; 1 Chron. 22:13) and New Testament (e.g., Mark 10:5; 12:26; Luke 2:22; 16:29, 31) refer to the Law of Moses as a distinct, authoritative source.

Old Testament passages also refer to written forms of prophetic oracles (Isa. 30:8; Jer. 25:13; 29:1; Ezek. 43:11; Dan. 7:1;

Hab. 2:2) and histories recorded by prophets (1 Chron. 29:29; 2 Chron. 9:29; 12:15; 13:22; 20:34). However, the first mention of a collection of biblical books is in Daniel 9:2, which suggests that by the time of Daniel, the book of Jeremiah was part of a larger collection of authoritative works that he calls "the books."

Later biblical writers make reference to earlier biblical books (2 Kings 14:6; 2 Chron. 25:4; 35:12; Ezra 3:2; 6:18; Neh. 8:1), and the prophets commonly rebuke the people for not obeying the words of previous prophets (Jer. 7:25; 25:4; Ezek. 38:17; Dan. 9:6, 10; Hos. 6:5; 12:10).

There is good evidence from Jewish tradition and other sources that the Jewish people believed that the prophetic voice ceased following the deaths of Haggai, Zechariah, and Malachi.[1] Therefore, it is likely that by about 300 BC the canon of the Old Testament was set in all its essentials. (See chap. 8.) While minor discussions about certain books continued well into the Christian era, they had little effect on the form of the Canon.

Jesus accepted the authority of the Hebrew canon and taught his disciples to reverence it (Matt. 5:17–18). The Christian church, which had its roots in the Jewish nation, maintained the same Hebrew canon (Matt. 23:34–35; Luke 11:50–51) and added the New Testament works to it.

How Were the Books Copied, and by Whom?

There are no remaining original manuscripts (commonly called "autographs") of the Old Testament, but there do exist an abundance of copies made by scribes whose only job was to preserve God's revelation. The autographs were probably written on scrolls made from papyrus or leather (see Jeremiah 36) that deteriorated from everyday use. When scrolls showed signs of wear, they were copied and reverently buried (since they contained

[1] *Tosefta, Sotah* 13.2; Babylonian Talmud, *Sotah* 48b, *Sanhedrin* 11a, and *Baba Bathra* 12a; *Seder Olam Rabbah* 30; Jerusalem Talmud, *Taanith* 2.1; *1 Macc.* 9:27; *Baruch* 85.3.

the sacred name of God). Sometimes worn copies were placed in a *genizah* ("hidden" place) until enough were gathered for a ritual burial ceremony. One of these *genizahs* was found in an old synagogue in Cairo around 1890.

Initially, priests (or a special group of priests) maintained the sacred traditions. Then, from about 500 BC to AD 100, an influential group of teachers and interpreters of the law arose, called the *soperim* ("scribes"), who meticulously copied and preserved the most accurate form of the Hebrew text that they could determine. The Babylonian Talmud states: "The older men were called *soperim* because they counted [Heb. *soper* may also mean "one who counts"] all the letters in the Torah."[2] There has been significant discussion as to what their early text looked like and how closely it corresponded to the modern Masoretic text (MT), the common form of today's Hebrew Bible, but it is not an easy question to answer.

Evidence from about the mid-third century BC and following indicates that a variety of Old Testament texts coexisted for several centuries (e.g., proto-MT [an early form of the Hebrew Masoretic text]; Greek Septuagint, a sometimes loose translation; Samaritan Pentateuch). Manuscripts copied before the first century AD show two tendencies on the part of the scribes: they preserved the accuracy of the text and, at the same time, they were willing to revise or update the specific words of the text. These tendencies are not contradictory—scribes assigned to the Scriptures a high degree of authority and upheld them with great reverence, but their desire was that readers understand them. Sometimes scribes intentionally changed texts because of things they felt were inappropriate or objectionable. Still, they carefully noted changes out of reverence for the text (e.g., in Judg. 18:30 scribes added the Hebrew letter *nun* above the line so that it read

---

[2] Babylonian Talmud, *Kiddushin* 30a.

"Manasseh" instead of "Moses" because Jonathan was acting more like a son of wicked Manasseh than of Moses).

A group of scribes called the *tannaim* (repeaters) maintained the sacred traditions from about AD 100 to 300 and developed meticulous rules to follow when copying synagogue scrolls (e.g., no word or letter was to be written from memory; if more than three mistakes were made on any page, it was destroyed and redone). While the text was reverenced and carefully maintained, it could be updated within specific, limited parameters: (1) By about 350 BC, texts had begun to be written in Assyrian (square) script instead of paleo-Hebrew. (2) Even before this, *matres lectionis* (Hebrew consonants added to a word to indicate how it should be pronounced—these were precursors to vowel points) were starting to be added and archaic spellings were modernized. (3) Some corrections were made.[3] It was common practice throughout the ancient Near East to update and revise texts.

Following the first century AD, however, the priority of scribes narrowed to preserving the accuracy of Scripture, which they did with amazing precision. Manuscripts dated to the first and second centuries AD (e.g., from Masada, Nahal Hever, Wadi Murabba'at, and Nahal Se'elim) reflect the proto-MT in orthography and content with very little variation. Debate continues over how and why the text became so unified following the first century AD. Some argue that the group who maintained the proto-MT was the only one to survive the destruction of the second temple. Others suggest there was a purposeful standardization of the text. The latter seems more likely for two reasons: (1) There was a desire to provide a consistent standard for debates between Christians and Jews in the first century AD;[4] (2) Hillel the Elder needed a

[3] See 4QIsaa.
[4] See Justin Martyr, *Dialogue* 68.

standardized text on which to base his seven rules of biblical hermeneutics.[5]

The sheer number of manuscripts, as well as quotations in rabbinic literature, suggest that the proto-MT was the primary text maintained by the authoritative center of Judaism. At the same time, other textual traditions were also circulated (e.g., Septuagint; Samaritan Pentateuch). However, sometime during the first century AD the proto-MT apparently became the dominant textual tradition.

Are the Texts Available Today an Accurate Reflection of the Originals?

To adequately answer this question requires some understanding of Old Testament textual criticism, which we will now briefly explore.

OLD TESTAMENT TEXTUAL CRITICISM

Scholars agree that no single witness perfectly reproduces the original Hebrew text (generally called "Urtext") of the entire Old Testament, and therefore textual criticism is necessary. *Textual criticism* is the science and art that seeks to determine the most reliable original wording of a text. It is a science because specific rules govern the evaluation of various types of copyist errors and readings, but it is also an art because these rules cannot be rigidly applied in every situation. The goal of Old Testament textual criticism is to work back as closely as possible to the final form of the text as it was canonized and maintained by the scribes. Since the texts were transmitted over such a long period, one could expect that minor errors might have crept in. Comparison of various forms of the Old Testament text helps determine the most plausible reading of the original texts. Intuition and common sense must guide this process. Informed judgments

[5] *Aboth of Rabbi Nathan* 37A.

about a text depend upon one's familiarity with copyist errors, manuscripts, versions, and their authors.

Types of Errors

Even given a strong desire to maintain an authoritative, standardized text, common copyist errors can creep in, including: confusion of similar letters, homophony (substitution of similar sounding letters or words), haplography (omission of a letter or word), dittography (doubling a letter or word), metathesis (reversal in the order of two letters or words), fusion (two words being joined as one), and fission (one word separated into two).

The Process

Modern critical editions of the MT include the *BHS* (*Biblia Hebraica Stuttgartensia*) and the *BHQ* (*Biblia Hebraica Quinta*), which follow the Codex Leningradensis (AD 1008), and the Hebrew University Bible Project, which follows the Aleppo Codex (c. 930). They derive from the longest and, to date, most reliable textual tradition overall. This tradition was maintained by the Masoretes, and when compared to the Qumran manuscripts dated about one thousand years earlier, was found to be very accurate. These critical editions also provide a summary of pertinent information from other sources in their textual apparatus. The process of Old Testament textual criticism includes examining the external evidence from various Hebrew sources (e.g., Dead Sea Scrolls, Samaritan Pentateuch, medieval manuscripts) and versions (e.g., Septuagint, Latin Vulgate, etc.) to determine which is the most plausible original reading of the text.

When weighing evidence, scholars generally agree that the Hebrew sources take precedence over the versions, though versions sometimes contain what appears as a plausible original reading. Internal evidence is then examined to see if there are any hints to help determine the original reading (e.g., grammatical structures, common spelling). At times, discoveries from other ancient Semitic languages have shed light on previously unintelligible texts. Guidelines to use in determining the most plausible original readings include: (1) Which reading could most likely give rise to the others? (2) Which reading is most appropriate in its context? (3) The weight of the manuscript evidence is then evaluated to determine whether it may contain a secondary reading or gloss. Only a very small percentage of the Hebrew text has any questionable readings, and of these only a small portion make any significant difference in the meaning of the text.

PRIMARY OLD TESTAMENT SOURCES

The following are the primary sources for present-day knowledge of the original Old Testament text:

Codex Leningradensis: The oldest complete copy of the MT, dated to AD 1008. Both the *BHS* and the *BHQ* follow this text.

Aleppo Codex: The oldest, incomplete copy of the MT, dated to about AD 930. About one-quarter of this manuscript was burned by fire, but its text is very similar to the Codex Leningradensis. The Hebrew University Bible Project uses this text as a base.

Dead Sea Scrolls: More than two hundred biblical manuscripts dated from about 250 BC to AD 135 from the area around the Dead Sea. The largest number of these texts agree closely with the readings of the proto-MT (35 percent of manuscripts) and help confirm the accuracy of the MT.

CONCLUSION

Although some textual puzzles remain, and though scholars still differ among themselves in how they weigh some of the evidence, careful application of these principles allows a high level of confidence that close access to the original texts does indeed exist.

Moreover, ordinary English readers should not suppose that there are hundreds of significant textual variants whose existence is known only to specialized scholars, for all the variants that translation teams thought to be significant for interpreting the text have been indicated in the footnotes of the ESV and other modern English translations. Looking through those footnotes will show a reader that the significant variants affect far less than 1 percent of the words of the ESV text, and even among that 1 percent, there are no variants that would change any point of doctrine. Therefore, while some places remain where it is hard to be sure of the original reading, as a general assessment it is safe to say that the Old Testament text that is the basis of modern English translations is remarkably trustworthy.

12

THE RELIABILITY
OF THE NEW TESTAMENT
MANUSCRIPTS

Daniel B. Wallace

Today, any group of Christians gathered together can all read exactly the same words in their Bibles. That luxury is made possible by the invention of the movable-type printing press over five centuries ago. But such a luxury can also breed a false sense of confidence that the precise original wording of the Bible can be known. When it comes to the New Testament, the original twenty-seven books disappeared long ago, probably within decades of their composition. Handwritten copies, or manuscripts, must be relied on to determine the wording of the original text. Yet no two manuscripts are exactly alike, and even the closest two early manuscripts have at least half a dozen differences per chapter (most of them inconsequential variations, however, as will be seen). The discipline known as New Testament textual criticism is thus needed because of these two facts: disappearance of the originals, and disagreements among the manuscripts.

But even though the original wording of the New Testament cannot be known, that fact is not necessarily cause for alarm. It is true that the New Testament manuscripts contain thousands of wording differences. It is also true that a few favorite passages are of dubious authenticity. But this is not the whole picture. Christians can, in fact, have a very high degree of confidence that what they have in their hands today is the Word of God.

This section's specific task is to (1) compare the number and antiquity of New Testament manuscripts with those of other ancient literature; (2) note the number and nature of the wording differences in the New Testament (including a discussion of a few of the more notable places in which the wording is in doubt); and (3) identify what is, and what is not, at stake in this discussion.

THE NUMBER AND ANTIQUITY OF NEW TESTAMENT MANUSCRIPTS COMPARED WITH OTHER ANCIENT LITERATURE

In comparison with the remaining manuscripts of any other ancient Greek or Latin literature, the New Testament suffers from an embarrassment of riches. It is almost incomprehensible to think about the disparity. When it comes to quantity of copies, the New Testament has no peer. More than 5,700 Greek New Testament manuscripts are still in existence, ranging in date from the early second century to the sixteenth century. To be sure, the earliest ones (i.e., through the third century) are all fragmentary, but they cover a substantial amount of the New Testament. And Greek manuscripts do not tell the whole story. The New Testament was translated early on into a variety of languages, including Latin, Coptic, Syriac, Armenian, Georgian, Gothic, and Arabic. All told, there are between twenty thousand and twenty-five thousand handwritten copies of the New Testament in various languages. Yet if all of these were destroyed, the New Testament text could be reproduced almost in its entirety by quotations of it in sermons, tracts, and commentaries written by ancient teachers of the church (known as church fathers or Patristic writers). To date, over a million quotations from the New Testament by the church fathers have been cataloged.

How does this compare with the average classical author? The copies of the average ancient Greek or Latin author's writings number fewer than *twenty* manuscripts! Thus, the New Testament has well over one thousand times as many manuscripts as the works of the average classical author.

When it comes to the temporal distance of the earliest copies of the New Testament from the original, New Testament textual critics again enjoy an abundance of materials. From ten to fifteen New Testament manuscripts were written within the first one hundred years of the completion of the New Testament. To be sure, they are all fragmentary, but some of them are fairly sizable fragments, covering large portions of the Gospels or Paul's letters, for example. Within two centuries, the numbers increase to at least four dozen manuscripts. Of manuscripts produced before AD 400, an astounding ninety-nine still exist—including the oldest complete New Testament, Codex Sinaiticus.

The gap, then, between the originals and the early manuscripts is relatively slim. By comparison, the average classical author has no copies for more than half a millennium.

Comparing the New Testament text to some better-known ancient authors, it still has no equal. Figure. 12.1 illustrates this by comparing the copies of five Greco-Roman historians' works with the New Testament. If one is skeptical about what the original New Testament text said, that skepticism needs to be multiplied many times over when it comes to the writings of all other ancient Greek and Latin authors. Although it is true that there are some doubts about the precise wording of the original in some places,

New Testament textual criticism has an unparalleled abundance of materials to work with, in terms of both quantity and age of manuscripts. Nothing else comes close.

Figure 12.1 Comparison of Extant Historical Documents

Histories	Oldest Manuscripts	Number Surviving
Livy 59 BC–AD 17	4th century AD	27
Tacitus AD 56–120	9th century AD	3
Suetonius AD 69–140	9th century AD	200+
Thucydides 460–400 BC	1st century AD	20
Herodotus 484–425 BC	1st century AD	75
New Testament	c. 100–150 AD	c. 5,700 (counting only Greek manuscripts) plus more than 10,000 in Latin, more than a million quotations from the church fathers, etc.

THE NUMBER AND NATURE OF THE WORDING DIFFERENCES

The Greek New Testament, as it is known today, has approximately 138,000 words. The best estimate is that there are as many as four hundred thousand textual variants among the manuscripts. That means that, on average, for every word in the Greek New Testament there are almost three variants. If this were the only piece of data available, it might discourage anyone from attempting to recover the wording of the original. But the large number of variants is due to the large number of manuscripts. Hundreds of thousands of differences among the Greek manuscripts, ancient translations, and patristic commentaries exist only because tens of thousands of such documents exist. Further, the vast majority of textual alterations are accidental and trivial, and hence easy for textual critics to spot.

These textual differences can be broken down into four categories. The largest group involves *spelling and nonsense errors*. The single most common textual variant involves what is known as a movable "nu." This is an "n" that is placed at the end of certain words when the next word begins with a vowel. The same principle is seen in English: *a* book, *an* apple. Nonsense errors occur when a scribe wrote a word that makes no sense in its context, usually because of fatigue, inattentiveness, or misunderstanding of the text in front of him. Some of these errors are quite comical, such as "we were *horses* among you" (Gk. *hippoi*, "horses," instead of ēpioi, "gentle," or *nēpioi*, "little children") in 1 Thessalonians 2:7 in one late manuscript.

The second-largest group of variant readings consists of *minor changes, including synonyms and alterations, that do not affect translation.* A common variation is the use of the definite article with proper names. Greek can say, "*the* Barnabas," while English translations will drop the article. The manuscripts vary in having the article or not. Word-order differences account for many of the variants. But since Greek is a highly inflected language, word order does not affect meaning nearly as much as it does in English. These two phenomena can be illustrated in a sentence such as "Jesus loves John." In Greek, that sentence can be expressed in at least sixteen different ways without affecting the basic sense. Factoring in spelling variations and other nontranslatable differences, "Jesus loves John" could, in fact, be a translation of hundreds of different Greek constructions. In this light, the fact that there are only three variants for every word in the New Testament, when the potential is seemingly infinitely greater, seems almost trivial.

The third-largest category of textual variants involves *meaningful changes that are not "viable."* "Viable" means that a variant has some plausibility of reflecting the wording of the original text. For example, in 1 Thessalonians 2:9, instead of "the gospel of *God*" (the reading of almost all the manuscripts), a late medieval copy has "the gospel of *Christ*." This is meaningful but not viable. There is little chance that one late manuscript could contain the original wording when the textual tradition is uniformly on the side of another reading.

The smallest category of textual changes involves *those that are both meaningful and viable*. These comprise less than one percent of all textual variants. "Meaningful" means that the variant changes the meaning of the text *to some degree*. It may not be terribly significant, but if the variant affects one's understanding of the passage, then it is meaningful. Most of these meaningful and viable differences involve just a word or a phrase. For example, in Romans 5:1, some manuscripts read "we have (Gk. *echomen*) peace," while others have "let us have (Gk. *echōmen*) peace." The difference in Greek is but a single letter, but the meaning is changed. If "we have peace" is authentic, Paul is speaking about believers' status with God; if "let us have peace" is authentic, the apostle is urging Christians to enjoy the experience of this harmony with God in their lives. As important as this textual problem is, neither variant contradicts any of the teachings of Scripture elsewhere, and both readings state something that is theologically sound.

There are two large textual variants in the entire New Testament, each involving twelve verses: Mark 16:9–20 and John 7:53–8:11. The earliest and best manuscripts lack these verses. In addition, these passages do not fit well with the authors' styles. Although much emotional baggage is attached to these two texts for many Christians, no essential truths are lost if these verses are not authentic.

Should the presence of textual variants, then, undermine the confidence of ordinary laypersons as they read the Bible in their own language? No—actually, the opposite is the case. The abundance of variants is the result of the very large number of remaining New Testament manuscripts, which itself gives a stronger, not weaker, foundation for knowing what the original manuscripts said.

In addition, modern Bible translation teams have not kept the location of major variants a secret but have indicated the ones they think to be most important in the footnotes of all "essentially literal" modern English translations, so that laypersons who read these footnotes can see where these variants are and what they say. The absence of any such footnote (which is the case with far more than 99 percent of the words in the English New Testament) indicates that these translation teams have a high degree of confidence that the words in their English translation accurately represent the words of the New Testament as they were originally written.

WHAT IS AT STAKE?

The most significant textual variants certainly alter the meaning of various verses. And where the meaning of verses is changed, paragraphs and even larger units of thought are also affected to some degree. At times, a particular doctrine may not, after all, be affirmed in a given passage, depending on the textual variant. But this is not the same thing as saying that such a doctrine is denied. Just because a particular verse may not affirm a cherished doctrine does not mean that that doctrine cannot be found in the New Testament. In the final analysis, no cardinal doctrine, no essential truth, is affected by any viable variant in the surviving New Testament manuscripts. For example, the deity of Christ, his resurrection, his virginal conception, justification by faith, and the Trinity are not put in jeopardy because of any textual variation. Confidence can therefore be placed in the providence of God in preserving the Scriptures.

In sum, although scholars may not be certain of the New Testament wording in a number of verses, for the vast majority of the words in the New Testament the modern English translations accurately represent what the original authors wrote, and therefore these translations can be trusted as reproducing the very words of God.

Part 5

ARCHAEOLOGY
AND THE BIBLE

13

ARCHAEOLOGY
AND THE RELIABILITY
OF THE OLD TESTAMENT

John Currid

DEFINITION OF ARCHAEOLOGY

"Archaeology" may be defined as *the systematic study of the material remains of human behavior in the past*. It includes written documents and objects of everyday life that are preserved in a fragile or ruined condition. In reality, as archaeologist Stuart Piggott famously remarked, archaeology is the "science of rubbish." Indeed, archaeologists spend their time and efforts in long-forgotten heaps of ancient refuse: broken pots, shattered buildings, and crumbling documents.

THE PURPOSE AND AIM OF ARCHAEOLOGY

The aim of archaeology is to discover, record, observe, and preserve the buried remains of antiquity and to use them to help reconstruct ancient life. In fact, archaeology is merely one of numerous disciplines that contribute to the understanding of ancient times and ways. Other fields, such as paleography and epigraphy (the study of ancient writing systems and inscriptions), history, linguistics, numismatics (the study of coins), and literature are also utilized to recover antiquity. Archaeology can paint only part of the picture; it is not exhaustive. For example, the site of Megiddo has been heavily excavated since the end of the nineteenth century, and yet only a slice of it has been unearthed. What archaeology provides for the reconstruction of ancient life at Megiddo is piecemeal and fragmentary. One cannot expect a complete picture through archaeology alone.

Archaeology in the lands of the Bible has a checkered past. It began in the mid-nineteenth century with Western pioneers who traveled throughout Palestine on horseback, compass in hand, attempting to identify and mark ancient sites from the time of the Bible. Actual excavation did not begin until the end of that century and, unfortunately, much of the work was no more than treasure hunting. The object often was to recover as many valuable relics as possible in the shortest time. Early archaeologists would not hesitate to use gunpowder to blast open a pyramid or a burial chamber. Mummy hunters in Egypt literally waded through piles of discarded coffins to reach their prey. Much has changed since those early days. Today excavation is systematic, scientific, and multidisciplinary.

Much of archaeology in the lands of the Bible focuses on sites that have been occupied for hundreds and even thousands of years. The site of Megiddo has occupational remains dating from the Neolithic period (c. 5000 BC) to the Persian period (fifth through fourth centuries BC). Such settlements are called "tells" (from the Arabic word; cf. Heb. *tel*, "heap, mound," Josh. 8:28; 11:13; Jer. 30:18; 49:2), which are artificial mounds. The first settlers would come to an area and build there, usually for three reasons: defense, a dependable water source, and a reliable food source. When the first settlement was destroyed by any of a number of causes, succeeding builders normally built a new settlement directly on top of the previous rubble. After each settlement, the mound would grow higher and thus be of greater strategic value. A tell, then, is like a layered cake in which each layer was put down sequentially, the most modern period being on top. The goal of the archaeologist is to disassemble in reverse the layers of the tell, and then to reconstruct the history and culture of the people who lived there—in other words, to dig up the story that is hidden in the mound.

Three primary categories of remains are uncovered through excavation: pottery, architecture, and various other small finds. Of the three, pottery is especially important for archaeology because of its durability and changeability. Pottery is found in every layer of a site because it lasts, and each layer has its own distinctive and typical pottery. By comparing pottery from different sites, archaeologists are able to derive a dating sequence and order for those locations.

THE RELATIONSHIP OF ARCHAEOLOGY TO THE BIBLICAL DISCIPLINES

No greater dilemma exists in archaeology in the land of the Bible than the question of what motivates excavation. What is the relationship of biblical studies to the scientific discipline of archaeology? What is the place of the scientific disciplines in archaeology? Is there a place for "biblical archaeology" today?

Historically, archaeology in Palestine has been uniquely the work of biblical scholars. Many of the archaeology pioneers of the nineteenth century were trained in and motivated by biblical studies. Edward Robinson (1794–1863), often considered the father of scientific topography and archaeology of Palestine, was primarily trained in Hebrew and the Old Testament. The first systematic excavators of Palestine were biblical scholars such as W. F. Albright, N. Glueck, and G. E. Wright. In the second half of the twentieth century, however, there was a loud call from the scientific community for a distinct separation between biblical studies and archaeological research. The argument was that the relationship between the two is largely artificial, and now it was time for archaeology to stand on its own as a scientific discipline. It is only natural, however, that the two disciplines work hand in hand because they are a source of knowledge and discovery for each other.

Today, a proper balance is necessary between archaeology in Palestine and biblical studies. While there have been some attempts to use archaeological finds to deconstruct ancient history and the life-setting of antiquity, the aim should rather be reconstruction: a harmonization in which biblical studies, archaeology, and other disciplines are used to recover and to understand the way people lived in the times and lands of the Bible. A prime purpose of archaeology is to shed light on the historical and material contexts in which the stories of the Bible took place. Thus, archaeology provides a life-setting for biblical texts. In that regard, archaeology can be a confirmatory tool, especially when the textual and archaeological evidence converge.

A good example of how archaeology illumines the Bible is the case of the Egyptian pharaoh Shishak and his invasion of Israel and Judah at the close of the tenth century BC. This attack is mentioned in 1 Kings 14:25–26: "In the fifth year of King Rehoboam, Shishak king of Egypt came up against Jerusalem. He took away the treasures of the house of the LORD and the treasures of the king's house. He took away everything." Extrabiblical sources confirm that this attack did take place, and they provide a wider understanding of it than what is recorded in the Bible. At the temple of Amun at Karnak, Shoshenk I (Shishak) built the Bubastite Portal, and on it appears a relief of Shishak's invasion of Palestine. The relief contains the names of various sites on the campaign route that were either captured or destroyed.

One conclusion that may be drawn from the Bubastite Portal is that Shishak's invasion of Palestine included more than a campaign against Jerusalem, and was leveled against the kingdoms of both Israel and Judah. Another important point is that Jerusalem is not mentioned on the relief. Why not? It is likely that it does not appear because it was not captured. King Rehoboam of Judah eluded Jerusalem's capture by paying heavy tribute to the Egyptians (as is recorded in 1 Kings 14:25–26). In this case, the biblical evidence illumines archaeological finds.

Archaeology provides even further insight into this invasion. One of the cities listed as either captured or destroyed by Shishak is Megiddo. At the site of Megiddo, excavators uncovered a stele (or inscribed pillar) of Shishak on which is written two common titles for Shishak. Stelae like this one were commonly set up by pharaohs to claim a region as a vassal (or subject) state. In addition, there is a "destruction layer" at Megiddo that can be associated with the campaign of Shishak. Further evidence for this association appears at the site of Ta'anach, where a huge destruction layer covered the site. The pottery sealed beneath the destruction is the same as that of the destruction layer at Megiddo. Ta'anach was also mentioned as a city subdued by Shishak in the relief of the Bubastite Portal. It is indeed compelling to relate the destruction layers at Ta'anach and Megiddo to the Shishak campaign of the late tenth century BC.

Archaeology complements both the Hebrew and Egyptian written sources as well in regard to the historical event of Shishak's invasion of Israel and Judah. A fuller picture of the event is painted by bringing these separate sources together. And this convergence is not unique: the biblical authors set events like the invasions of Sennacherib and Nebuchadnezzar in their proper chronological framework and setting (see 2 Kings 18:13;

19:16; 24:1–10; 1 Chron. 6:15; 2 Chron. 32:1–22). These events are confirmed and filled out by contemporary ancient Near Eastern texts—the prism of Sennacherib for the former campaign, and the Lachish Letters for the latter. Excavation work has also brought to light numerous destruction layers at Judean sites that reflect both of those campaigns.

As for the bearing of archaeological study on the historical reliability of the Old Testament, what has been the result of many decades of archaeological investigation? The answer is simple: archaeology has time and again supported and confirmed the biblical record.

14

ARCHAEOLOGY AND THE RELIABILITY OF THE NEW TESTAMENT

David W. Chapman

Christians have often looked to archaeology to provide confirmation of the biblical record, which it indeed can. Yet the main advantage of archaeology lies in its ability to bring twenty-first-century readers into physical contact with the cultures in which Jesus and his apostles lived and ministered.

ARCHAEOLOGICAL METHODOLOGY

Archaeology today stands at the intersection of science and the humanities. Gone are the days when the amateur could take a spade and go hunting for treasures. Modern archaeology requires careful procedures, meticulous recording techniques, and a vast array of scientific technologies. Yet after all the data has been accumulated, the most interesting jobs entail interpreting the evidence.

Excavations at New Testament cities often uncover large structures such as monuments, tombs, and buildings (whether residential, civic, or commercial). These can be quite interesting, yet the smaller finds are often equally (if not more) illuminating. Such small finds include inscriptions, coins, papyri, figurines, and day-to-day artifacts (e.g., pottery, glass, furniture, and remnants of clothing). Visual art (such as mosaics, frescoes [paintings on moist plaster], friezes [carved reliefs], and statuary) can reveal many aspects of ancient life—from dress to social and religious practices.

Archaeological digs proceed slowly, layer by layer, in well-marked squares in order to understand each square's relative chronology. Written records, drawings, and photographs accompany every square. While sophisticated dating procedures can be employed (such as radiocarbon), the primary techniques of dating archaeological strata typically still rely on pottery finds (both their form and their fabric) or on datable coins and inscriptions. The type of building can be identified by its architectural style, but this may not yield results as precise as those provided by the firmer dates of coins and inscriptions. Most dating methods require some degree of interpretation. It is important to realize that many excavated structures and artifacts from a city may stem from a time before or after the New Testament; although these can still be pertinent to understanding the cultures of the apostolic period, caution should be employed when correlating them with the New Testament.

Because the complete excavation of a large site can take many decades, knowledge of most ancient places is limited. For example, even though the ancient cities of Jerusalem, Rome, Ephesus, and Corinth have each been under excavation for over a century, much remains to be done in all of them. Thus, there should be caution concerning arguments from silence (claiming that because something has not been found, it does not exist). Furthermore, excavations have historically focused on the monumental architecture of those who were rich, while smaller residential structures (often constructed of short-lasting materials) may be underrepresented.

INTERPRETING ARCHAEOLOGICAL FINDS

When there are varying opinions about a discovery, these usually occur at the level of interpretation. One of the initial interpretative acts of an excavator concerns "site identification"—discovering the ancient name of a known archaeological site. The identification of a particular locale synthesizes modern local traditions, ancient written sources, and the actual finds at that place (especially inscriptions and coins). Sometimes biblical sites are hard to find, or more than one possibility exists. For example, both Cana (John 2:1) and Bethany across the Jordan (John 1:28) have more than one possible location. Fortunately, most New Testament towns are fairly well identified.

Particular architectural features within towns also require identification. Structures such as theaters and stadiums are fairly obvious, and baths have special features (such as particular heating systems), but understanding the use of other buildings may be complex. For example, the architecture of temples is often straightforward, but determining which deity was worshiped where can be difficult (e.g., the great temple in Corinth has been variously identified with Apollo or Athena). What was the purpose of a given civic building? Which set of shops in Corinth housed the meat market? In some cases, ancient literary sources may help (such as Pausanias's *Description of Greece*, essentially a second-century AD tour guide), but often interpretation involves intricate arguments based on specific features.

Even ancient inscriptions can raise questions. Do any of the extant Sergius Paulus inscriptions relate to the governor of Cyprus in Acts 13:7? How does one interpret the unusual Greek reference to the "place of the Jews who also fear God" in Miletus (see Acts 20:17)? At times a name appears, such as the name "Caiaphas" on the side of a richly decorated ossuary (Jewish bone reburial box), and the identification with a New Testament person seems probable (see John 18:24). On other occasions, some media personalities are too quick to correlate ancient finds with New Testament figures. Many names mentioned in the New Testament were common, such as the Jewish names Jesus, Joseph, Mary, James, and Matthew. Thus, when someone claims that the bones of Jesus Christ have actually been found in one of a few extant Jerusalem ossuaries labeled "Jesus son of Joseph," skepticism is warranted, given that hundreds of people would have been so named in antiquity.

Certainly, archaeology involves scientific methods, but archaeological interpretation also requires professional competencies and a good bit of wisdom. Perhaps the best advice for those interested in archaeology would be to encourage them to read reliable sources and not to rely heavily on exciting new finds reported first in the popular media.

ARCHAEOLOGY AND THE HISTORICITY
OF THE NEW TESTAMENT

Many historical features of the New Testament can be supported from the archaeological record, and in fact one overwhelming result of archaeological research into the New Testament period has been to give strong confirmation to the New Testament writings' historical accuracy. For example, the Gospel of John evidences an amazingly accurate awareness of the geography of Palestine. John's descriptions of ancient Samaria have been confirmed by archaeology, including

Samaritan worship on Mount Gerizim (4:20) and the location of Jacob's well (4:6). Concerning Jerusalem, John's Gospel carefully depicts the pool of Bethesda (5:2) and Solomon's colonnade (10:22–23), which archaeology has been able to authenticate. Also, discoveries in 2005 helped confirm John's portrayal of the pool of Siloam (9:7).

The book of Acts has been shown to well represent the geography of antiquity. Nearly every town in the book has been identified, and many cities have been excavated. The Acts record of Paul's travels to Rome, including his shipwreck, presents one of the most detailed and useful travel accounts from antiquity (Acts 27). Luke, the author of Acts, even knows the correct terms for specific governors—as shown by uncovered inscriptions mentioning the proconsul Gallio (18:12), the asiarchs of Ephesus (19:30–31), and the politarchs of Thessalonica (17:1, 6).

Many other examples could be cited of historical aspects of the New Testament also found in the archaeological record. Inscriptions mention New Testament figures such as Pontius Pilate (Luke 23:1) and Herod the Great (Matt. 2:1). The synagogue of Capernaum has been found beneath another structure from late antiquity (Mark 1:21). Crucifixions were performed with nails, as the Gospels indicate (John 20:25), and such nails survive. The cities addressed in Revelation 2–3 often have historical features that line up well with aspects of their biblical description.

Furthermore, archaeology occasionally provides the scholar with new discoveries of biblical manuscripts. Archaeologists are partially responsible for the fact that there are now thousands of Greek manuscripts of the New Testament and even more manuscripts of early New Testament translations. All these manuscripts, some from a time close to the age of the apostles, have made the New Testament the best-attested set of writings from antiquity (see chap. 12).

ARCHAEOLOGY AND NEW TESTAMENT CULTURAL CONTEXTS

A fuller understanding of the meaning of the New Testament can be achieved by learning more about the world in which its human authors and recipients lived. Biblical interpretation begins with understanding the original meaning of each passage before applying it to one's contemporary life or situation. The original meaning was targeted toward people in particular cultures; the better those cultures are understood, the more accurately the New Testament can be interpreted. Archaeology can assist in this cultural understanding. In fact, while archaeological finds occasionally confirm the historicity of the New Testament, archaeological discoveries regularly provide insights into ancient culture. Moreover, archaeology serves as a reminder that New Testament events occurred in real time-space history.

If one were to tour with Paul the great Roman-era cities of his day, familiar features would appear at every juncture, and these can be reimagined with the aid of recent excavations. The shops and markets indicate a general prosperity in the cities. The civic structures show the power of Rome yet also suggest how it often worked through local governments. The theaters and odeions (buildings for music and recitations) testify to artistic endeavors, as do the many works of mosaic, fresco, and sculpture. The stadiums and their hero sculptures boast of athletic achievement. Baths, gymnasiums, and latrines evidence both the cultural aspiration to cleanliness and the training of youth. And all these theatrical, artistic, athletic, and civic functions were intricately tied to the cults of the pagan religions. More than anything, the modern reader would probably be shocked at how many pagan religious structures (from small niches to monumental temples) are found at seemingly every turn.

Inscriptions that exhibit Jewish symbols, names, and synagogue references significantly illustrate the great expanse of the Jewish Diaspora (Jews living outside the land of Palestine) throughout the Mesopotamian and Mediterranean world. Many synagogues have been found both inside and outside of Palestine. Jewish cultic objects, inscriptions, and other excavated remains increasingly reveal the complex interplay that existed between Jew and Gentile in Galilee. From Judea, Samaria, and Galilee, the structures of Jesus's day are being unearthed.

Aspects of daily life can be understood by examining everything from the most mundane pot to the huge homes of the elite (whether in Jerusalem, Pompeii, or Ephesus). Christians adapted some homes to serve as churches (1 Cor. 16:19). Clothing and personal aesthetics are displayed in art and are attested in the occasional preserved find (such as two-thousand-year-old sandals from the Judean desert). Pottery, glass, furniture, and other artifacts help explain how people lived. Animal bones, ancient seeds, and farm tools reveal agricultural practices. Coins illustrate rulers and the symbols they valued.

Ancient tombs testify to views of death. The Roman world had a range of burial practices—from cremation, to shallow graves, to family cave-tombs, to monumental mausoleums. Some Jewish family tombs clearly employed rolling stones as doors (see Mark 15:46). Jewish people would reuse their burial niches, and around Jerusalem they might rebury the skeletons in ossuaries (reburial boxes). People were often buried alongside cultural objects (perhaps viewed as special to a person or as needed in the life to come)—these tomb remains are frequently some of the best-preserved small objects from any excavation. Modern osteologists analyze excavated skeletons for such matters as age, gender, general health, and cause of death.

Papyri (such as those from Oxyrhynchus or Tebtunis) provide ancient letters and legal documents not otherwise passed down in the literary record. These give a "behind-the-scenes" view into how people lived. Other excavated writings allow access to previously unknown literature. Especially important have been texts from post–New Testament Gnosticism (found at Nag Hammadi) and the extensive collection of Jewish manuscripts from Qumran, Masada, Nahal Hever, and Murabbaat.

More could certainly be said about how archaeology has enhanced the knowledge of the cultures in which New Testament people lived. Yet this chapter should suffice to show that archaeology, in addition to its significant contribution in supporting the historical reliability of the New Testament, renders an even greater service by inviting readers into the world of Jesus and his followers.

Part 6

THE ORIGINAL LANGUAGES OF THE BIBLE

15

HEBREW AND ARAMAIC, AND HOW THEY WORK

Peter J. Williams

The main language of the Old Testament is Classical Hebrew, but some parts are in Aramaic (Ezra 4:7–6:18; 7:12–26; Jer. 10:11; Dan. 2:4–7:28). Two words of Aramaic also occur in the place name *Jegar-sahadutha* in Genesis 31:47.

The form of Hebrew found in the Bible was probably spoken from as early as 1500 BC to some time after 400 BC. Although Aramaic (the official international language of the Assyrian, Babylonian, and Persian Empires) came increasingly into daily use among Jews, many Jews (at least in the Jerusalem area) continued to use a form of Hebrew (which later developed into "Mishnaic" Hebrew, the language of the Mishnah). Hebrew documents with varying degrees of similarity to Biblical Hebrew have been found at Qumran and in the desert of Judah, with dates from the second century BC to the second century AD.

The synagogues in Palestine retained the use of Hebrew as a sacred language. Modern Hebrew, which was developed in the late nineteenth and early twentieth centuries, is based on the earlier forms of Hebrew and is one of the official languages of the modern state of Israel (founded in 1948).

Both Hebrew and Aramaic are part of the wider family of languages that since 1781 have been labeled "Semitic," a name derived from that of Noah's son *Shem*. However, languages from this group were also spoken by some peoples (such as the Amorites, Babylonians, and Canaanites) that Genesis does not record as being descended from Shem.

SEMITIC LANGUAGES

While there are many Semitic languages, they can generally be organized according to the three regions where they were spoken: (1) East Semitic (Mesopotamia), including Old Akkadian, Assyrian, and Babylonian; (2) South-West Semitic (parts of northeastern Africa), including North Arabic (the language of the Qur'an) and Ethiopian; and (3) North-West Semitic (Syro-Palestine), including Amoritic and Ugaritic, along with Hebrew, Phoenician, Moabite (the Canaanite branch), and Aramaic and Syriac (the Aramaic branch). When considered together, the Semitic languages have a longer continuous history of being written than almost any other group.

Alphabet

Hebrew, Aramaic, and some neighboring Semitic languages share an alphabet of twenty-two consonant letters only (twenty-three if the *sin* and *shin* are counted separately) and are read from right to left. The shape and order of these Hebrew characters had been distilled by the second millennium BC, before the time of Moses (and the writing of the Old Testament). This alphabet was then passed by way of the Phoenicians to the Greeks, while the Hebrew and Aramaic forms of the script began to diverge. The form of Hebrew script generally used until at least the Babylonian exile, and still found in some Dead Sea Scrolls, is known as the Paleo-Hebrew script. Some of its letters still resemble their equivalents in the Greek alphabet. During the rule of the Persians (539–332 BC) the square Aramaic (or Assyrian) script was adopted for writing Hebrew, with the result that the forms of letters originally used for Aramaic are now almost universally associated in people's minds with Hebrew (see fig.15.1).

The alphabet itself has had an effect on the form of certain texts in the Old Testament. A number of the Psalms (Psalms 9; 10; 25; 34; 37; 111; 112; 119; 145) are arranged as types of acrostic poems composed around the twenty-two letters of the Hebrew alphabet, as are the first four chapters of Lamentations.

MATRES LECTIONIS

In order to give further precision to pronunciation of words, and to clarify ambiguities between words that shared the same consonants, three of the consonant letters came to be used to represent vowels. The letter *h* (ה) represented *a* or *e*; *w* (ו) represented *o* or *u*, and *y* (י) represented *e* or *i*. In inscriptions from biblical times, these *matres lectionis* (Latin for "mothers of reading," i.e., "vowel letters") were rare before the exile, and it is therefore often held that preexilic biblical writings that display extensive use of *matres lectionis* had these letters added after the time of composition to help readers understand the words properly. It is still the case, however, that earlier texts, such as the Pentateuch, are more sparing in the use of these than, for example, postexilic writings such as the books of Chronicles.

ROOTS

Semitic words are generally based on so-called roots consisting of three consonants. Vowels and a limited range of other consonants are arranged around these roots to produce words. Consider the following Hebrew words:

melek ("king")
malkah ("queen")
mamlakah ("kingdom")
malak ("he reigned")
malkut ("reign")

The constant element in all of these words is the consonant sequence *m-l-k*, which is associated with royal rule. Sometimes a particular word may occur only once in the whole Old Testament, and the question naturally arises as to how its meaning is known. If, however, there are other words from the same root, its meaning can be identified in relation to them (with due consideration given also to its context).

MASORETIC POINTING

The Old Testament writings were produced using consonants only. Pronunciation was possible by adding vowel sounds to the consonantal words, and thus the particular vocalization and accentuation of Biblical Hebrew was understood aurally, and was therefore taught and memorized and passed down to each successive generation orally through the Jewish schools and synagogues.[1] However, as Biblical Hebrew was no longer in use as a spoken language among the Jews, and in order to avoid ambiguities in the text by ensuring that the correct pronunciation was not lost, Jewish textual scholars between the fifth and eighth centuries AD devised and inserted into the Old Testament text a system of vowel points to guide readers in how the words should be correctly vocalized and accented. These Jewish scribes, known as the Masoretes (from the Heb. *masorah*, "what was

---

[1] Cf. the anecdote in Babylonian Talmud, *Baba Bathra* 21a–b.

Fig. 15.1 Hebrew Alphabet

Hebrew name	Square (Assyrian or Aramaic) script	Paleo-Hebrew form	Sound	Traditional transliteration
Aleph	א	ⵊ	glottal stop	ʾ
Beth	ב	ⴹ	b	b
Gimel	ג	⌐	g	g
Daleth	ד	△	d	d
He	ה	ⴺ	h	h
Waw	ו	ⵝ	w	w
Zayin	ז	ⵏ	s	z
Heth	ח	ⴲ	ch ("loch")	ḥ
Teth	ט	⊗	t	ṭ
Yod	י	ⵘ	y	y
Kaph	כ, ך	ⴘ	k	k
Lamedh	ל	ⵐ	l	l
Mem	מ, ם	ⴸ	m	m
Nun	נ, ן	ⴹ	n	n
Samekh	ס	ⵣ	s	s
Ayin	ע	○	–	ʿ
Pe	פ, ף	ⴶ	p	p
Tsadhe	צ, ץ	ⵕ	ts	ṣ
Qoph	ק	ⴼ	q	q
Resh	ר	ⴰ	r	r
Sin	שׂ	w	s	ś
Shin	שׁ	w	sh	š
Taw	ת	✕	t	t

141

handed down," i.e., "tradition"), applied this system of "pointing" by adding marks (dots and strokes) around the consonants without disturbing or changing any of them. The Masoretes thus "pointed" the Hebrew text of the Old Testament with symbols indicating vowel sounds so that the traditional way Scripture had been read and heard in the synagogues would be preserved even though Biblical Hebrew was ceasing to be spoken among the Jewish people. Here is an example of the word "king" in unpointed and pointed form:

Unpointed	מלך	mlk
Pointed	מֶלֶךְ	melek

In addition to providing guidance as to which vowels occur within a word, the Masoretic pointing also distinguishes between different pronunciations of the same letter. The so-called *begad-kephath* letters—*b*, *g*, *d*, *k*, *p*, and *t*—also had the spirant (or fricative) pronunciations *bh*, *gh*, *dh*, *kh*, *ph*, and *th*. A single dot (called a *daghesh*) inside the letter (e.g., בּ) would specify the "hard" pronunciation *b* rather than the "soft" pronunciation *bh* (ב), etc. By the position of a point, Masoretic notation also distinguished two different sounds that lay behind the Hebrew letter שׁ. Hebrew שׂ represented *s* (*sin*) and שׁ represented *sh* (*shin*). Medieval Hebrew manuscripts also contain a further set of marks known as accents or cantillation signs, which indicate division and cohesion in the text and specify the way the text should be sung in the synagogue.

Masoretes actively worked in three areas—Babylon, Palestine, and Tiberias. Eventually it was the tradition from Tiberias (called Tiberian vocalization), particularly the work of the Ben Asher family in Tiberias (c. AD 900), that came to be preserved in the Hebrew Bible today (i.e., the Masoretic text [MT]; thus also the *Biblia Hebraica Stuttgartensia* [BHS]). However, a further guide to the historical pronunciation of words is available in the tradition of pronunciation of the Pentateuch among the Samaritans. On the surface, the Samaritan pronunciation usually seems rather different from the Tiberian vocalization. Yet when historical sound changes are taken into account, it often shows regular correspondence to that of the Masoretes.

VERBAL SYSTEM

Almost all Hebrew verbs are built upon three root or stem consonants (alluded to above), though these will rarely appear in the text without an accompanying affix of some kind. There are seven main stem formations (or *binyanim*) of Hebrew verbs: *Qal*, *Niphal*, *Piel*, *Pual*, *Hithpael*, *Hiphil*, and *Hophal*. Each of these seven divisions convey something different about the relationship between the subject and the verbal action (active, passive, reflexive, causative, etc.), and these are apparent by the characteristic changes that the same three-consonant verbal stem undergoes within each division (though most verbs do not occur in all seven stem formations).

The many structural differences between Hebrew and English influence translation. Whereas English has a system of verbal *tenses* (i.e., time of action—past, present, future, etc.), many grammarians prefer to say that Hebrew has two verbal *aspects* (i.e., kind of action—complete, incomplete) known as the perfect and imperfect. In the simplest terms, these aspects consider actions as either complete or incomplete, respectively. Thus, the Hebrew imperfect is frequently used for referring both to events in the future and to repeated events in the past. A further complication is the relationship that the perfect and the imperfect verb have with the conjunction "and" (Hebrew letter *waw*). When *waw* (ו) attaches as a prefix to a perfect or imperfect verb, it may at times appear to reverse the function of the perfect or imperfect aspect so that the perfect then communicates incomplete action and the imperfect communicates complete action, even if, from a historical perspective, this is not actually what is happening (it actually preserves an old tense form). Such differences between the Hebrew and English verbal systems can make translation difficult at times. However, in most prose texts, the temporal location of the narrative is immediately clear and, consequently, so is the way in which one should render a passage. Poetic texts are more complex, but there is still a surprising agreement between English translations as to which tense to use.

THE *WAW* PARTICLE

Closely connected with the verbal system is the ubiquity of *waw* (ו; "and") in the Hebrew Bible. It is used to begin books with no previous connection with another narrative (e.g., Esther, Ezekiel, Jonah) and is the main particle connecting clauses in prose texts. Although Hebrew has some particles that carry senses such as "but," "therefore," and "because," these words are less commonly used than *waw*, which in connection with various clauses can be rendered by a range of terms. The ESV, for example, renders *waw* by the neutral "and" where appropriate, but also uses words such as "now" (Judg. 2:1), "so" (Judg. 2:14), "then" (Judg. 2:16), and "but" (Judg. 2:19) when the context calls for it.

PREPOSITIONS

Hebrew also has fewer prepositions than English, with the result that the same Hebrew preposition can be rendered in a variety of ways. For instance, renderings of the preposition *b* (ב) may include "in," "on," "by," and "with." Hebrew has no word for "of," but the possessive and other relationships expressed by English "of" can be represented in Hebrew by using the "construct state." In the construct state, a noun is placed immediately before another noun in an inseparable (attached) position. Sometimes this involves a change in the form of the first noun as it loses stress. Thus, the underlined word is in the construct state in the following examples: *melek* ("king") + *yisra'el* ("Israel") → *melek yisra'el* ("king *of* Israel"); *malkah* ("queen") + *yisra'el* ("Israel") → *malkat yisra'el* ("queen *of* Israel").

ARTICLES
Hebrew has a definite article: *h* (ה) precedes the noun, usually with a short *a*-vowel (ַ) and doubling of the initial consonant of the noun. There is no indefinite article in Biblical Hebrew. Thus *melek* means "king" or "a king," but *hammelek* means "the king." In poetic texts, however, the definite article is used more sparingly, and it is therefore sometimes legitimate to use a definite article in translating a Hebrew phrase that lacks one (as in the ESV rendering "in the scroll of the book," in Ps. 40:7).

GENDER AND NUMBER
Hebrew has two genders (masculine and feminine) and three numbers (singular, dual, and plural). The dual is used only to refer to two items that occur in a pair (e.g., "eyes," "knees," "teeth," "millstones"). Verbs and pronouns also distinguish between a masculine and a feminine form of the second person ("you") in singular and plural forms, and between a masculine and a feminine form of the third-person plural ("they"). The distinction between the genders of the pronouns plays a significant part in the ESV identification of speakers in the Song of Solomon (see, e.g., ESV footnote on Song 1:11).

DIVERSITY
The Hebrew of the Old Testament is not uniform. Certain songs, such as the Song of Deborah (Judges 5) and the Song of Moses (Ex. 15:1–18), display archaic linguistic features. Though there is still a strong underlying linguistic unity to the Old Testament, the language found throughout the thirty-nine books shows that

the Old Testament was composed over a considerable period of time. Moreover, the language of the Old Testament also reflects dialectal differences (see Judg. 12:6). Occasionally, features of certain Old Testament texts are identified by scholars as coming from the northern kingdom (Israel), as opposed to Judah, for example.

ARAMAIC

The term "Aramaic" comes from the people of Aram (an ancient region of upper Mesopotamia), the Arameans, whom Old Akkadian writings mention as early as the third millennium BC. During the eighth and seventh centuries BC, the Assyrian Empire controlled much of the ancient Near East, and Aramaic spread in usage as an international language (see 2 Kings 18:26; Isa. 36:11) until the Persian Empire of the sixth century BC established it as the official language. The few Aramaic sections of the Old Testament (Gen. 31:47; Ezra 4:8–6:18; 7:12–26; Jer. 10:11; Dan. 2:4–7:28) fit clearly within the category of Imperial Aramaic, the language of Persian administration. Much of the grammatical description of Biblical Hebrew given above could, with minor changes, also apply to Aramaic. Eventually, Aramaic came into daily use with many Jews, especially those in Galilee. Aramaic words appear in the New Testament on the lips of Jesus (e.g., Mark 5:41; 7:34), and the name Golgotha (Mark 15:22) is Aramaic in form. The term of respectful address, 'abba', seems also to be Aramaic, but it became standard in later Hebrew as well. The expression *ephphatha* ("be opened!" Mark 7:34) may be Aramaic, though some think it is the equivalent form in Hebrew. Paul uses the Aramaic expression *marana tha* ("our Lord, come!") in 1 Corinthians 16:22.

CONCLUSION

While Biblical Hebrew enjoyed over one thousand years of existence as a spoken language—from the middle of the second millennium BC until the close of the BC era—it has never truly "died" but continues to thrive today through the perpetual study and translation of the writings of the Old Testament Scriptures. Furthermore, it is still actively spoken and used in Jewish religious life and synagogues around the world. It is taught and passed down in both Christian seminaries and Jewish yeshivas. And because of its use by God as the language of the Old Testament, it will continue to enjoy a detailed preservation and rich textual tradition virtually unparalleled by any other ancient language.

16

GREEK, AND HOW IT WORKS

David Alan Black

BACKGROUND

Starting in May of 334 BC, Alexander, the twenty-one-year-old
king of Macedon, led his victorious army through four pitched
battles, two sieges, and innumerable smaller engagements that
enabled him to conquer territory that now goes under the names
of Turkey, Syria, Lebanon, Israel, Egypt, Iraq, Iran, and Afghani-
stan. Reaching the banks of the Beas River in Pakistan, he reluc-
tantly turned back as his exhausted troops threatened mutiny.
Three years later, in 323 BC, he died (at age thirty-two) in Babylon, just as he was planning an expedition all the way from
Egypt along the North African coast to the Atlantic.

When Alexander died, his empire broke up into separate
kingdoms headed by his disgruntled generals. But he had changed
the world. In the old, now liberated cities of Asia Minor—
Ephesus and Pergamum—as well as in the newly founded cities
of the Middle East—Antioch and Alexandria—the culture and

language of the colonial aristocracy was Greek. Three centuries after Alexander's death, when the life and teaching of Jesus of Nazareth was written down, the language used was not Jesus's native Aramaic but Greek, which, thanks to Alexander's conquests, had become the common language of the Mediterranean world. The conclusion now universally accepted by philologists is that the Greek of the New Testament, in all essential respects, is the vernacular Koine of the first century AD, the language of the Roman imperial period.

KOINE GREEK

Koine means "common" in the sense of pertaining to the public at large. Hence, "Koine Greek" means the language commonly spoken everywhere—the basic means of communication of people throughout the Roman Empire. This dialect was basically the late Attic vernacular, spoken in Athens, with dialectal and provincial influences. In addition to the Greek New Testament, the Koine has left other literary monuments that are invaluable sources of light on the sacred text, including papyri, inscriptions, the writings of numerous Jewish and early Christian authors, and above all the Septuagint, the ancient version of the Old Testament that became the Bible of the early church and was used extensively by the New Testament writers.

Koine Greek itself exhibits three important characteristics. The first, *semantic change*, is a natural feature of any language. The meanings of certain words were weakened in the Koine period. For example, the noun *dōma* meant "house" or "room" in Classical Greek, but in the New Testament it came to mean "roof" of a house (Luke 5:19). In the New Testament the preposition *eis* can mean "in" as well as "into," though it meant only "into" in Classical Greek. The conjunction *hina* has a much wider meaning in Koine than "in order that," which was the meaning in Classical Greek. For instance, *hina* is often used in content clauses simply to mean "that." The tendency in Koine to use the comparative degree of the adjective for the superlative may also be noted. Second, Koine Greek exhibits *greater simplicity* than Classical Greek. This is seen primarily in the composition of its sentences, which tend toward coordination rather than subordination of clauses. Finally, Koine Greek shows unmistakable traces of a tendency toward *more explicit* (some would say more redundant) *expression*, as seen, for example, in the use of pronouns as subjects of verbs and the use of prepositional phrases to replace simple cases. Adverbs abound, as do parenthetical statements and emphatic expressions such as "each and every" and "the very same."

At the same time, Koine Greek was not entirely uniform. Various literary levels existed, depending on the writer's background, education, or even sources. In the first century AD, some writers even attempted to turn back the clock by advocating a return to the old classical form of Greek, decrying the Koine as a debased form of the language. The artificial style they produced (called "Atticistic" Greek) contrasted with the dialect of everyday life.

STYLES OF GREEK IN THE NEW TESTAMENT

The New Testament itself reveals several styles of Greek among its authors. The highly literary epistle to the Hebrews, with its careful progression of argument and elevated diction, lies at one extreme. Luke and Acts also reveal good literary style, though the author (Luke) is able to vary his style considerably (cf. the colloquial Greek of Peter's speech in Acts 15:7–11 with the rhetorical nature of Paul's Areopagus speech in Acts 17:22–31, or the Classical introduction in Luke 1:1–4 to the more Septuagintal style of Luke 1:5–2:52). Paul's Greek is more or less colloquial, but that may be partly due to his amanuenses, the secretaries who wrote from his dictation. At the other end of the spectrum lies the grammar of Revelation, which may reflect the work of a Semitic-speaking person who lacks a polished knowledge of Greek (though many of the idioms John uses have direct parallels in colloquial papyri texts).

GREEK LINGUISTICS

Greek linguistics has emerged as one of the most fundamental disciplines in biblical studies—as important, for example, as the study of molecular physics in the natural sciences. Biblical scholars have recently become concerned with the problems of language to a degree equaled only in the early history of modern comparative linguistics, when New Testament scholars such as Deissmann and Moulton began demolishing the myth of "Holy Ghost" Greek (the belief that God created a special language in which to inscripturate the New Testament). Today several scholars are specifically interested in what they call the "semantics of biblical language."

It is a central concern of semantics that a clear distinction be maintained between words as linguistic units and the concepts associated with them. All languages have several ways of expressing a concept, and rarely does a concept consist of only one word. This confusion of word and concept is one of the chief faults of Kittel's *Theological Dictionary of the New Testament*. In treating words as if they were concepts, it incorrectly implies that the words themselves contain the various theological meanings assigned to them. But the meanings of words are determined from the way they are used in context. There is now consensus that interpreters must work at the level of the paragraph to discern meaning.

The capacity of a word to have two or more meanings is technically known as *polysemy*—a particular form of a word can belong to different fields of meaning, only one of which need be its semantic contribution to a single sentence or context. The principle of polysemy is frequently ignored in exegesis, leading to what is called the fallacy of "illegitimate totality transfer," which occurs when the various meanings of a word in different contexts are gathered together and then all those meanings are presumed to be present in any single context. For example, it would be illegitimate to presume without further indication that in any single passage the word *ekklēsia* must refer to the church, the body of Christ. In Acts 7:38, for example, "church" (in the New Testament sense) would clearly *not* be the author's meaning and would actually be contradictory to the sense of the passage.

Another important linguistic concept is *synonymy*. Synonymy can be considered the opposite of polysemy: in synonymy, two or more words may be associated with the same meaning, whereas in polysemy two or more meanings are associated with the same word. A biblical example of synonymy involves the Greek vocabulary for "love." The relationship between the meanings of *agapaō* and *phileō* is such that the words may be used interchangeably in some contexts. One thereafter need not be surprised that *agapaō* (popularly considered to refer to divine love) can describe Amnon's incestuous relationship with his half-sister Tamar (2 Sam. 13:15, LXX) or that *phileō* (popularly taken to refer to a lower form of love) can refer to the Father's love for the Son (John 5:20). Other New Testament examples of synonymy are *logos/rhēma* ("word"), *horaō/blepō* ("I see"), and *oida/ginōskō* ("I know"). In each case, according to the principle of "semantic neutralization," any of the terms in these pairs may in some contexts be used interchangeably without any significant difference in meaning, depending on the purpose of the biblical author. (Smaller differences in nuance or connotation, however, are often still present among synonyms.)

GREEK AS AN INFLECTED LANGUAGE

Greek is a highly inflected language (like its contemporary, Latin). This means that most Greek words undergo changes in keeping with their function in the sentence in which they occur. For example, Greek nouns have five basic cases (or sets of forms): nominative, vocative, genitive, dative, and accusative. (English still bears a faint resemblance to this trait in such words as "dog," "dogs," "dog's," and "dogs'," or in "I" and "he" used as subjects, "me" and "him" used as objects, and "my" and "his" used to show possession.) Because Greek word inflections designate the function of each word in its sentence, Greek allows much more variation in word order than English does, for example, where a different word order often changes the meaning. In addition, Greek verbs function within an extensive and highly developed system of tenses, voices, moods, gender, and number, giving modern Greek students considerable consternation, but providing flexibility for a very broad range of nuances of meaning. Koine Greek's linguistic stock (the set of words available for use) was incredibly rich, and new words could easily be coined by combining older words or adding a variety of common prefixes. These features all made Koine Greek a wonderfully resourceful language with a remarkable ability to express an author's meaning precisely and understandably.

THE IMPORTANCE OF STUDYING GREEK TODAY

Is this ancient language worth studying today? Yes, indeed! The many tools available can give modern readers the knowledge and understanding to incorporate Greek into their own life and ministry, and into their personal Bible study. A knowledge of Greek will probably not make a reader think that the meaning of a verse is completely different from that indicated in a reliable, essentially literal modern translation, but it will certainly give the reader the ability to understand the meaning more precisely, to decide more accurately among various nuances that might be allowed by the English text, to understand why many popular interpretations are incorrect, and to have deeper confidence in knowing the precise sense of the verse. Meanwhile, those who will never learn Greek can still be thankful for scholars who have studied it extensively and who have prepared modern English translations that make available to the reading public an accurate rendering of what the original says.

17

THE SEPTUAGINT

Peter J. Gentry

The term "Septuagint" is commonly used today to refer to the Greek translation of the Jewish Scriptures, the books that are called the "Old Testament" in Christian terminology. Scholars who specialize in Septuagint studies point out, however, that in a more technical sense the word "Septuagint" refers only to the Greek translation of the Pentateuch. Uncertainties about the history of the process of translation are responsible for the variation in meaning of the term.

It is generally agreed that the Pentateuch (Genesis–Deuteronomy) was translated in Egypt early during the reign of Ptolemy II Philadelphus (285/282–246 BC), possibly around 280 if one can rely on the testimony of the church fathers. The books in the Prophets and Writings were translated later, certainly most of them by 130 BC as is indicated by the prologue to the Greek translation of *Sirach* (*Ecclesiasticus*). Questions arise about the date of translation of each of the books in the collection known as Megilloth (Ruth, Song of Solomon, Ecclesiastes, Lamentations, and Esther). Some of these may have been first translated after 100 BC.

To complicate matters further, long before all the books had been translated, revisions were already being made of existing translations. The process of making systematic, thoroughgoing revisions (called recensions) continued from possibly 200 BC through AD 200. The precise line of demarcation between original translations and revisions in this body of texts has not yet been clearly established. Scholars are still working to prepare editions of these translations based on careful study of all available evidence in Greek manuscripts, citations by church fathers, and early daughter translations.

THE MOTIVATION FOR THE TRANSLATION

What motivated the translation of the Septuagint continues to be debated. Five major hypotheses have been advanced: (1) A generation of Greek-speaking Jews in the Hellenistic period begun by the conquest of Alexander the Great (333–323 BC) required Greek Scriptures for their religious life and liturgy and/or (2) for the education of their young. (3) The translation was required as a legal document or (4) as cultural heritage for the royal library being assembled in Alexandria. (5) Aristarchus's new edition of Homer around 150 BC employed textual criticism to produce an authoritative text, and this served as an incentive and a model to produce an authoritative text of the Bible for Alexandrian Jews (hence early revisions and *The Letter of Aristeas*).

THE ORIGIN OF THE SEPTUAGINT

A document known as *The Letter of Aristeas* purports to relate the story of the origin of the Greek Pentateuch. This document is actually a propaganda piece, written in 150–100 BC to authenticate the Greek version in the face of criticisms circulating at that time—criticisms to the effect that the Greek translation did not adequately reflect the Hebrew text current in Palestine.

The name Septuagint comes from *septuaginta*, the Latin word for "seventy." (The common abbreviation for the Septuagint is LXX, the Roman numeral for seventy.) According to *Aristeas*, there were seventy-two translators. The number seventy is an adaptation of seventy-two based on models like the seventy Elders at Sinai, the seventy Judges who assisted Moses, the seventy Elders of the Sanhedrin, etc. Likely there were just five translators for the Pentateuch, as rabbinic versions of the story indicate.[1] While church fathers like Justin Martyr (c. AD 135) refer to the seventy translators, the earliest use of the term Septuagint as a reference to the translation itself is found in Eusebius's *Ecclesiastical History* (c. AD 303).

DIFFERENT TRANSLATION APPROACHES WITHIN THE SEPTUAGINT

In both ancient and modern times, different approaches to the task of translation have been adopted. Each language employs its words as a code to "cut up" and represent the "pie" of reality. The code of one language may overlap with that of another in multiple ways or perhaps not at all in some aspects. Just as light may be refracted as a continuum of colors on a spectrum, so translations may be characterized as a continuum on a spectrum from highly literal (sometimes called formal equivalence) to functional equivalence (also called dynamic equivalence).

At one end of the spectrum translations can be woodenly literal, simply translating item for item, word for word, even copying the word order of the original language in ways that make the translation sound unnatural. The code of the receptor language is conformed as closely as possible to that of the source language. Then further along the spectrum are "essentially lit-

[1] *Aboth of Rabbi Nathan* 37; *Soferim* 1.7.

eral" translations that seek to render the meaning of each word in the original but to do so in contextually sensitive ways and to produce a readable, natural-sounding translation. *Functional equivalence*, at the other end of the spectrum, is dynamic, idiomatic, idea for idea or "thought for thought," so to speak. The code of the *receptor* language (even when it differs significantly from the original language) is followed as closely as possible to maximize effective communication and understanding for the audience.

Thus different notions of fidelity in transmitting the Word of God motivate the different ends of the spectrum. When the codes of source and target languages overlap in multiple ways, often more than one correct translation of an expression is possible. For example, if the source language specifies a relationship of possession between the nouns "Mary" and "purse," there are a number of right ways to say this: "Mary's purse," "the purse of Mary," "the purse that belongs to Mary," "the purse that Mary has," etc. The books in the Greek Pentateuch as well as those in the Prophets and Writings vary widely within this spectrum of types of translation. Some are literal in the extreme; others are more idiomatic and represent various gradations of functional equivalence.

Genesis and Exodus in the Septuagint range from essentially literal to fairly dynamic translations, while Leviticus, Numbers, and Deuteronomy are quite literal. The translator of the book of Job abbreviated many of the long, windy speeches for his Hellenistic readership so that the book is one-sixth shorter in Greek. The translator of Proverbs rearranged the material to enhance the figure of Solomon. Other books, such as Esther and Daniel, have additions to them. The Septuagint version of Jeremiah for some reason differs significantly from the Hebrew text in both arrangement and text. Most of the books, however, reflect the same Hebrew text preserved in the Masoretic text.

The differences between the Septuagint and the later standard Hebrew text (the Masoretic text) are due to a number of factors. In some cases, the translators were using a Hebrew parent text that differs somewhat from the Masoretic text. In most cases, differences are due simply to a different way of reading the same text or understanding the grammar and meaning of words.

The Septuagint quickly became popular among the Jews of the Diaspora for whom Greek was the familiar spoken language. When the Christian church began to spread beyond Jewish borders, they adopted the Septuagint as their ordinary Bible, with minor modifications (while still recognizing that it was a translation). For example, the book of Daniel in the Septuagint was considered so deficient by the Christian church that they rejected it, and in its place used a later Greek translation attributed to Theodotion.

Many of the quotations of the Old Testament in the New Testament are from the Septuagint, or even early revisions of it, and as a result differ from the Masoretic text. The differences range from superficial to significant. Sometimes the "quotations" are not actually quotations in a modern sense but are the New Testament author's modification and adaptation of the Septuagint wording to apply to a new circumstance (see, e.g., Acts 4:11, borrowing words from Ps. 118:22; and 2 Cor. 6:18a, borrowing from 2 Sam. 7:14). At other times the New Testament authors correct the Septuagint reading, bringing it closer to the Hebrew (e.g., 1 Cor. 14:21, using Isa. 28:11–12; and Eph. 4:30, using Isa. 63:10).

Differences due to copyist errors in textual transmission and variations in translation do not in any way weaken the strong claim made by Jesus and the apostles concerning the inspiration and accuracy of the Scriptures. They affirmed the divine authority both of the Old Testament itself and of their own writings as they at various times used and adapted both the Masoretic text and some of the readings found in copies of the Septuagint. The differences and variations in the texts were there in Jesus's time just as they are today. No doubt in many cases the New Testament authors were aware of the differences but were able to use them for their own purposes. This does not imply that they thought the Septuagint always represented the wording of the documents as originally written, but only that they affirmed the truthfulness of the words they quoted or adapted to the new context of their own writing.

REVISIONS OF THE SEPTUAGINT

Before the end of the first century AD, Jews were reacting against the use of the Septuagint, partly because it did not reflect current rabbinic teaching and partly because of Christian apologetics based on the Septuagint, not only where it was accurate but even sometimes where it had faulty renderings. Therefore, the Jews produced a number of revisions of the Septuagint to make it conform to the Hebrew text more closely. The most important of these were by Theodotion (50 BC–AD 50; literal), Aquila (c. AD 120; extremely literalistic), and Symmachus (c. 180; dynamic). Almost all later translations of the Old Testament (Old Latin, Syro-Hexapla, Coptic, Armenian, Ethiopic, Arabic, Gothic, Old Georgian, Old Slavic) were made from the Septuagint rather than directly from the Hebrew. (But the Syriac Peshitta version and the Latin Vulgate made extensive use of a Hebrew text, and the Samaritan Pentateuch was itself a Hebrew text.)

Christian codices (plural of "codex," which is an early kind of book consisting of bound sheaves of handwritten pages) of the Bible from the fourth/fifth century AD contain additional books beyond the thirty-nine books of the Old Testament and twenty-seven books of the New Testament. Some of these additional books are translations of Hebrew originals, but most were originally written in Greek. These books represent Jewish literature written between 300 BC and AD 100 and were called the Apocrypha by Jerome. (See chap. 10.) Some have mistakenly thought that these books were included by Alexandrian Jews in their canon. Yet Judaism in Alexandria was not independent of Palestinian Judaism, as even *Aristeas* reveals.

Not all of the books of the Apocrypha were originally composed in Greek or even in Egypt. Moreover, *1 Maccabees*, one of the books of the Apocrypha, acknowledged that inspiration had ceased (*1 Macc.* 4:46; 9:27; 14:41) before it was written. The prologue to *Sirach* (c. 130 BC) does not seem to include the Apocrypha as Scripture, and Philo, who ought to be a key source of information on Alexandria, does not quote the Apocrypha. Nor did he write commentaries on these books, even though he wrote on all the books in the Hebrew canon. Since the extant manuscripts of the Septuagint are of Christian, not Jewish, origin and are copies made five hundred years after the original translations, the great uncial codices (early codices written entirely with capital letters called "uncials") cannot be guides as to what was canonical in Alexandria in the third century BC. The books of the Apocrypha were not considered inspired by either Jews or Christians, but were popular reading among both groups.

THE IMPORTANCE OF THE SEPTUAGINT

The Septuagint is important for many reasons. First, the Septuagint represents an extremely early text of the Old Testament. Our oldest complete manuscripts of the Hebrew Old Testament date to c. AD 1000, and even the portions of the Old Testament found in the Dead Sea Scrolls date from around 200 BC to AD 68. But the Septuagint translation of the Pentateuch was done in the third century BC. To the extent that we can use it to determine the Hebrew text from which it was translated, we have a much older testimony to the text of the Old Testament. (On the other hand, the Hebrew Masoretic text is the result of an extremely careful process of copying and transmission and often represents a more accurate preservation of the original wording than that found in the Septuagint, although this can be decided only on a case-by-case basis. At times the Septuagint better preserves the more original wording.) And in spite of some variations, the Septuagint usually shows the same text later preserved in the Masoretic text. Since the Septuagint predates the Dead Sea Scrolls and is complete while they are fragmentary, it is more important than the Dead Sea Scrolls as a textual witness.

Second, the Greek Old Testament, as a translation, gives us an extremely early understanding of difficult points of grammar in the Hebrew text and the meanings of Hebrew words otherwise unknown to us.

Third, since all translation involves interpretation, the Greek Old Testament is, in effect, the earliest commentary on the Hebrew text.

Fourth, since the Greek Old Testament was produced between the end of the Old Testament and the beginning of the New Testament, it represents a key witness to the thought and worldview of Second Temple Judaism (c. 516 BC–AD 70).

Fifth, the Greek translation was often used by the apostles when quoting the Old Testament in the New Testament and was adopted early on as the ordinary Bible of the Christian church. Understanding the language of the Greek Old Testament is key to understanding the Greek of the New Testament. The Septuagint affected the language of the apostles just as the King James Version has influenced the vocabulary of Christians in our time. Such influence is especially evident in the writings of Luke, who contributed more to the New Testament than Paul in amount of text. For example, in the parable of the good Samaritan (Luke 10) Jesus asks who was a neighbor to the man who fell among thieves. An expert in the Torah answers, "the one who did 'mercy' with him." The expression is as strange in Greek as in English, but comes by way of the Septuagint from the expression in Hebrew for performing acts of kindness that demonstrate and fulfill covenant loyalty and love.

Finally, the history of the Greek Old Testament bears witness to debates over approaches to translation and to the problem of variations in the text of the Bible at the time of Jesus. This can shed some light on debates over similar topics today.

For these reasons, the study of the Greek Old Testament can be of great value to the church today.

Part 7

OLD TESTAMENT
AND NEW

18

A SURVEY OF THE HISTORY OF SALVATION

Vern S. Poythress

How does the Bible as a whole fit together? The events recorded in the Bible took place over a span of thousands of years and in several different cultural settings. What is their unifying thread?

One unifying thread in the Bible is its divine authorship. *Every book of the Bible is God's word*. The events recorded in the Bible are there because God wanted them recorded, and he had them recorded with his people and their instruction in mind: "For whatever was written in former days was written for our instruction, that through endurance and through the encouragement of the Scriptures we might have hope" (Rom. 15:4).

GOD'S PLAN FOR HISTORY
The Bible also makes it clear that *God has a unified plan for all of history*. His ultimate purpose, "a plan for the fullness of

time," is "to unite all things in him [Christ], things in heaven and things on earth" (Eph. 1:10), "to the praise of his glory" (Eph. 1:12). God had this plan even from the beginning: "Remember the former things of old; for I am God, and there is no other; I am God, and there is none like me, declaring the end from the beginning and from ancient times things not yet done, saying, 'My counsel shall stand, and I will accomplish all my purpose' " (Isa. 46:9–10). "When the fullness of time had come," when the moment was appropriate in God's plan, "God sent forth his Son, born of woman, born under the law, to redeem those who were under the law" (Gal. 4:4–5).

The work of Christ on earth, and especially his crucifixion and resurrection, is the climax of history; it is the great turning point at which God actually accomplished the salvation toward which history had been moving throughout the Old Testament. The present era looks back on Christ's completed work but also looks forward to the consummation of his work when Christ will come again and when there will appear "new heavens and a new earth in which righteousness dwells" (2 Pet. 3:13; see Rev. 21:1–22:5).

The unity of God's plan makes it appropriate for him to include *promises and predictions* at earlier points in time, and then for the *fulfillments* of these to come at later points. Sometimes the promises take *explicit* form, as when God promises the coming of the Messiah, the great Savior whom Israel expected (Isa. 9:6–7). Sometimes the promises take *symbolic* form, as when God commanded animal sacrifices to be offered as a symbol for the forgiveness of sins (Leviticus 4). In themselves, the animal sacrifices were not able to remove sins permanently and to atone for them permanently (Heb. 10:1–18). They pointed forward to Christ, who is the final and complete sacrifice for sins.

CHRIST IN THE OLD TESTAMENT

Since God's plan focuses on Christ and his glory (Eph. 1:10–12), it is natural that the promises of God and the symbols in the Old Testament all point forward to him. "For all the promises of God find their Yes in him [Christ]" (2 Cor. 1:20). When Christ appeared to the disciples after his resurrection, his teaching focused on showing them how the Old Testament pointed to him: "And he said to them, 'O foolish ones, and slow of heart to believe all that the prophets have spoken! Was it not necessary that the Christ should suffer these things and enter into his glory?' And beginning with Moses and all the Prophets, he interpreted to them in all the Scriptures the things concerning himself" (Luke 24:25–27). One could also look at Luke 24:44–48: "Then he said to them, 'These are my words that I spoke to you while I was still with you, that everything written about me in the Law of Moses and the Prophets and the Psalms must be fulfilled.' Then he opened their minds to understand the Scriptures, and said to them, 'Thus it is written, that the Christ should suffer and on the third day rise from the dead, and that repentance and forgiveness of sins should be proclaimed in his name to all nations, beginning from Jerusalem. You are witnesses of these things.'"

When the Bible says that "he opened their minds to understand *the Scriptures*" (Luke 24:45), it cannot mean just a few scattered predictions about the Messiah. It means the Old Testament as a whole, encompassing all three of the major divisions of the Old Testament that the Jews traditionally recognized. "The Law of Moses" includes Genesis to Deuteronomy. "The Prophets" include both the "former prophets" (the historical books Joshua, Judges, 1–2 Samuel, and 1–2 Kings) and the "latter prophets" (Isaiah, Jeremiah, Ezekiel, and the Twelve Minor Prophets, Hosea–Malachi). "The Psalms" is representative of the third grouping by the Jews, called the "Writings." (The book of Daniel was placed in this group.) At the heart of understanding all these Old Testament books is the truth that they point forward to the suffering of Christ, his resurrection, and the subsequent spread of the gospel to "all nations" (Luke 24:47). The Old Testament as a whole, through its promises, its symbols, and its pictures of salvation, looks forward to the actual accomplishment of salvation that took place once for all in the life, death, and resurrection of Jesus Christ.

THE PROMISES OF GOD

In what ways does the Old Testament look forward to Christ? First, it directly points forward through *promises of salvation and promises concerning God's commitment to his people.* God gave some specific promises in the Old Testament relating to the coming of Christ as the Messiah, the Savior in the line of David. Through the prophet Micah, God promises that the Messiah is to be born in Bethlehem, the city of David (Mic. 5:2), a prophecy strikingly fulfilled in the New Testament (Matt. 2:1–12). But God often gives more general promises concerning a future great day of salvation, without spelling out all the details of how he will accomplish it (e.g., Isa. 25:6–9; 60:1–7). Sometimes he promises simply to be their God (see Gen. 17:7).

One common refrain is that, "I will be their God, and they shall be my people" (Jer. 31:33; see also Hos. 2:23; Zech. 8:8; 13:9; Heb. 8:10). Variations on this broad theme may sometimes focus more on the people and what they will be, while at other times they focus on God and what he will do. God's promise to "be their God" is really his comprehensive commitment to be with his people, to care for them, to discipline them, to protect them, to supply their needs, and to have a personal relationship with them. If that commitment continues, it promises to result ultimately in the final salvation that God works out in Christ.

The principle extends to all the promises in the Old Testament. "For all the promises of God find their Yes in him [Christ]"

(2 Cor. 1:20). Sometimes God gives immediate, temporal blessings. These blessings are only a foretaste of the rich, eternal blessings that come through Christ: "Blessed be the God and Father of our Lord Jesus Christ, who has blessed us in Christ with every spiritual blessing in the heavenly places" (Eph. 1:3).

WARNINGS AND CURSES

God's relation to people includes not only blessings but also warnings, threatenings, and cursings. These are appropriate because of God's righteous reaction to sin. They anticipate and point forward to Christ in two distinct ways. First, *Christ is the Lamb of God, the sin-bearer* (John 1:29; 1 Pet. 2:24). He was innocent of sin, but became sin for us and bore the curse of God on the cross (2 Cor. 5:21; Gal. 3:13). Every instance of the wrath of God against sin, and his punishments of sin, looks forward to the wrath that was poured out on Christ on the cross.

Second, *Christ at his second coming wars against sin and exterminates it.* The second coming and the consummation are the time when the final judgment against sin is executed. All earlier judgments against sin anticipate the final judgment. Christ during his earthly life anticipated this final judgment when he cast out demons and when he denounced the sins of the religious leaders.

COVENANTS

The promises of God in the Old Testament come in the context not only of God's commitment to his people but also of instruction about the people's commitment and obligations to God. Noah, Abraham, and others whom God meets and addresses are called on to respond not only with trust in God's promises but with lives that begin to bear fruit from their fellowship with God. The relation of God to his people is summed up in various *covenants* that God makes with people. A covenant between two human beings is a binding commitment obliging them to deal faithfully with one another (as with Jacob and Laban in Gen. 31:44). When God makes a covenant with man, God is the sovereign, so he specifies the obligations on both sides. "I will be their God" is the fundamental obligation on God's side, while "they shall be my people" is the fundamental obligation on the human side. But then there are variations in the details.

For example, when God first calls Abram, he says, "Go from your country and your kindred and your father's house to the land that I will show you" (Gen. 12:1). This commandment specifies an obligation on the part of Abram, an obligation on the human side. God also indicates what he will do on his part: "And I will make of you a great nation, and I will bless you and make your name great, so that you will be a blessing" (Gen. 12:2). God's commitment takes the form of promises, blessings, and curses. The *promises and blessings* point forward to Christ, who is the fulfillment of the promises and the source of final blessings. The *curses* point forward to Christ both in his bearing the curse and in his execution of judgment and curse against sin, especially at the second coming.

The obligations on the human side of the covenants are also related to Christ. Christ is fully man as well as fully God. As a man, he stands with his people on the human side. He fulfilled the obligations of God's covenants through his perfect obedience (Heb. 5:8). He received the reward of obedience in his resurrection and ascension (see Phil. 2:9–10). The Old Testament covenants on their human side thus point forward to Christ's achievement.

By dealing with the wrath of God against sin, Christ changed a situation of alienation from God to a situation of peace. He reconciled believers to God (2 Cor. 5:18–21; Rom. 5:6–11). He brought personal intimacy with God, and the privilege of being children of God (Rom. 8:14–17). This intimacy is what all the Old Testament covenants anticipated. In Isaiah, God even declares that his servant, the Messiah, will be the covenant for the people (see Isa. 42:6; 49:8).

OFFSPRING

It is worthwhile to focus on one specific element in Old Testament covenants, namely, the promise concerning offspring. In making a covenant with Abram, God calls on him to "walk before me, and be blameless" (Gen. 17:1). That is a human obligation in the covenant. On the divine side, God promises that he will make Abram "the father of a multitude of nations" (Gen. 17:4), and he renames him Abraham (Gen. 17:5). The covenant with Abraham in fact extends beyond Abraham to his posterity: "And I will establish my covenant between me and you and *your offspring after you* throughout their generations for an *everlasting* covenant, to be God to you and to your offspring after you. And I will give to you and to your offspring after you the land of your sojournings, all the land of Canaan, for an everlasting possession, and I will be their God" (Gen. 17:7–8).

The promises made to Abraham are exceedingly important within the Old Testament because they are the foundation for the nation of Israel. The history after Abraham shows that Abraham had a son, Isaac, in fulfillment of God's promise to Sarah. Isaac was the immediate result of God's promise of offspring who will inherit the land. Isaac in turn had a son, Jacob, and Jacob was the father of twelve sons who in turn multiplied into the twelve tribes of Israel. The nation of Israel became the next stage in the offspring that God promised.

But how does this relate to Christ? Christ is the descendant of David and of Abraham, as the genealogy in Matthew indicates (Matt. 1:1). Christ is the offspring of Abraham. In fact, he is the offspring in a uniquely emphatic sense: "Now the promises were made to Abraham and to his offspring. It does not say, 'And to offsprings,' referring to many, but referring to one, 'And to your offspring,' *who is Christ*" (Gal. 3:16; cf. Gen. 22:15–18).

Abraham was told to "walk before me, and be blameless" (Gen. 17:1). Abraham was basically a man of faith who trusted

175

God (Gal. 3:9; Heb. 11:8–12, 17–19). But Abraham also had his failures and sins. Who will walk before God and be blameless in an ultimate way? Not Abraham. Not anyone else on earth either, except Christ himself (Heb. 4:15). All the other candidates for being "offspring" of Abraham ultimately fail to be blameless. Thus the covenant with Abraham has an unbreakable tie to Christ. Christ is the ultimate offspring to whom the other offspring all point. One may go down the list of offspring: Isaac, Jacob, then the sons of Jacob. Among these sons, Judah is their leader who will have kingship (Gen. 49:10). David is the descendant of Abraham and Judah; Solomon is the descendant of David; and then comes Rehoboam and the others who descend from David and Solomon (Matt. 1:1–16).

Christ is not only the descendant of all of them by legal right; he is also superior to all of them as the uniquely blameless offspring. Through Christ believers are united to him and thereby themselves become "Abraham's offspring" (Gal. 3:29). Believers, Jews and Gentiles alike, become heirs to the promises of God made to Abraham and his offspring: "There is neither Jew nor Greek, there is neither slave nor free, there is no male and female, for you are all one in Christ Jesus. And if you are Christ's, then you are Abraham's offspring, heirs according to promise" (Gal. 3:28–29).

CHRIST AS THE LAST ADAM

Christ is not only the offspring of Abraham, but—reaching back farther in time to an earlier promise of God—the offspring of the woman: "I will put enmity between you [the serpent] and the woman, and between your offspring and her *offspring*; he shall bruise your head, and you shall bruise his heel" (Gen. 3:15). The conquest over the serpent, and therefore the conquest of evil and the reversal of its effects, is to take place through the offspring of the woman. One can trace this offspring down from Eve through Seth and his godly descendants, through Noah, and down to Abraham, where God's promise takes the specific form of offspring for Abraham (see Luke 3:23–38, which traces Jesus's genealogy all the way back to Adam). Thus Christ is not only the offspring of Abraham but also the last Adam (1 Cor. 15:45–49). Like Adam, he represents all who belong to him. And he reverses the effects of Adam's fall.

SHADOWS, PREFIGURES, AND "TYPES"

The New Testament constantly talks about Christ and the salvation that he has brought. That is obvious. What is not so obvious is that the same is true of the Old Testament, though it does this by way of *anticipation*. It gives us "shadows" and "types" of the things that were to come (see 1 Cor. 10:6, 11; Heb. 8:5).

For example, 1 Corinthians 10:6 indicates that the events the Israelites experienced in the wilderness were "examples for us." And 1 Corinthians 10:11 says, "Now these things happened to them as an example, but they were written down for our instruction, on whom the end of the ages has come." In 1 Corinthians 10:6 and 11, the Greek word for "example" is *typos*, from which derives the English word "type" (cf. Rom. 5:14).

A "type," in the language of theology, is *a special example, symbol, or picture that God designed beforehand, and that he placed in history at an earlier point in time in order to point forward to a later, larger fulfillment*. Animal sacrifices in the Old Testament prefigure the final sacrifice of Christ. So these animal sacrifices were "types" of Christ. The temple, as a dwelling place for God, prefigured Christ, who is the final "dwelling place" of God, and through whom God comes to be with his people (Matt. 1:23; John 2:21). The Old Testament priests were types of Christ, who is the final high priest (Heb. 7:11–8:7).

Fulfillment takes place preeminently in Christ (Eph. 1:10; 2 Cor. 1:20). But in the New Testament those people who are "in Christ," who place their trust in him and experience fellowship with his person and his blessings, receive the benefits of what he has accomplished, and therefore one can also find anticipations or "types" in the Old Testament that point forward to the New Testament church, the people in the New Testament who belong to Christ. For example, the Old Testament temple not only prefigured Christ, whose body is the temple (John 2:21), but prefigured the church, which is also called a temple (1 Cor. 3:16–17), because it is indwelt by the Holy Spirit. Some Old Testament symbols also may point forward especially to the consummation of salvation that takes place in the new heaven and the new earth yet to come (2 Pet. 3:13; Rev. 21:1–22:5). Old Testament Jerusalem prefigured the New Jerusalem that will come "down out of heaven from God" (Rev. 21:2).

CHRIST THE MEDIATOR

The Bible makes it clear that ever since the fall of Adam into sin, sin and its consequences have been the pervasive problem of the human race. It is a constant theme running through the Bible. Sin is rebellion against God, and it deserves death: "The wages of sin is death" (Rom. 6:23). God is holy, and no sinful human being, not even a great man like Moses, can stand in the presence of God without dying: "You cannot see my face, for man shall not see me and live" (Ex. 33:20). Sinful man needs a *mediator* who will approach God on his behalf. Christ, who is both God and man, and who is innocent of sin, is the only one who can serve: "There is one mediator between God and men, the man Christ Jesus, who gave himself as a ransom for all" (1 Tim. 2:5–6).

Though there is only one mediator in an ultimate sense, in a subordinate way various people in the Old Testament serve in some kind of mediatorial capacity. Moses is one of them. He went up to Mount Sinai to meet God while all the people waited at the bottom of the mountain (Exodus 19). When the people of Israel were terrified at hearing God's audible voice from the mountain, they asked for Moses to bring them God's words from then on (Ex. 20:18–21). God approved of the arrangement involving Moses bringing his words to the people (Deut. 5:28–33).

But if there is only one mediator, as 1 Timothy 2:5 says, how could Moses possibly serve in that way? Moses was not the ultimate mediator, but he *prefigured* Christ's mediation. Because Moses was sinful, he could not possibly have survived the presence of God without forgiveness, that is, without having a sinless mediator on his own behalf. God welcomed Moses into his presence only because, according to the plan of God, Christ was to come and make atonement for Moses. The benefits of Christ's work were reckoned beforehand for Moses's benefit. And so it must have been for all the Old Testament saints. How could they have been saved otherwise? God is perfectly holy, and they all needed perfection. Perfection was graciously reckoned to them because of Christ, who was to come.

That means that *there is only one way of salvation*, throughout the Old Testament as well as in the New Testament. Only Christ can save us. "And there is salvation in no one else, for there is no other name under heaven given among men by which we must be saved" (Acts 4:12). The instances of salvation in the Old Testament all depend on Christ. And in the Old Testament, salvation frequently comes through a *mediator*, a person or institution that stands between God and man. All the small instances of mediation in the Old Testament prefigure Christ. How else could it be, since there is only one mediator and one way of salvation?

So understanding of the unity of the Bible increases when one pays attention to *instances where God brings salvation, and instances where a mediator stands between God and man*. These instances include not only cases where God brings spiritual salvation in the form of personal fellowship, spiritual intimacy, and the promise of eternal life with God. They also include instances of *temporal*, external deliverance—"salvation" in a physical sense, which prefigures salvation in a spiritual sense. And indeed, salvation is not *merely* spiritual. Christians look forward to the resurrection of the body and to "new heavens and a new earth in which righteousness dwells" (2 Pet. 3:13). Personal salvation starts with renewal of the heart, but in the end it will be comprehensive and cosmic in scope. The Old Testament, when it pays attention to physical land and physical prosperity and physical health, anticipates the physicality of the believer's prosperity in the new heavens and the new earth.

Instances of mediators in the Old Testament include prophets, kings, and priests. *Prophets* bring the word of God from God to the people. *Kings*, when they submit to God, bring God's rule to bear on the people. *Priests* represent the people in coming before God's presence. Christ is the final prophet, king, and priest who fulfills all three functions in a final way (Heb. 1:1–3). One can also look at *wise men*, who bring God's wisdom to others; *warriors*, who bring God's deliverance from enemies; and *singers*, who bring praise to God on behalf of the people and speak of the character of God to the people.

Mediation occurs not only through human figures, but through institutions. *Covenants* play a mediatorial role in bringing God's word to the people. The *temple* brings God's presence to the people. The *animal sacrifices* bring God's forgiveness to the people. In reading the Bible one should look for ways in which God brings his word and his presence to people through means that he establishes. All these means perform a kind of mediatorial role, and because there is only one mediator, it is clear that they all point to Christ.

19

HOW THE NEW TESTAMENT QUOTES AND INTERPRETS THE OLD TESTAMENT

C. John Collins

As C. S. Lewis once observed, "one of the rewards of reading the Old Testament regularly" is that "you keep on discovering more and more what a tissue of quotations from it the New Testament is."[1] Conscientious readers of the Bible may well acknowledge this; but there is much disagreement among New Testament interpreters on just *how* the New Testament authors saw the Old Testament from which they quoted. Questions include: Did the New Testament authors respect the original meaning of the Old Testament texts? Did they put new meanings into these Old Testament texts, and if so, how closely tied were these new meanings to the original meaning? Did a citation of

---

[1] C. S Lewis, *Reflections on the Psalms* (New York: Harcourt, Brace, 1958), 26.

an Old Testament passage invoke the whole context of the Old Testament passage, or was the New Testament writer really only interested in what he could make a particular "verse" do for him? What kind of text did the New Testament authors use: the original Hebrew, or the Septuagint, or another Greek version—and did the New Testament authors depend on the Greek, even when its rendering of the Hebrew was inadequate?

This short chapter cannot supply a complete discussion of all these questions, nor does it suggest that all faithful interpreters see things the same way. Rather, the aim here is to offer a way of looking at these issues that does justice both to the New Testament and to the Old Testament.

A VARIETY OF KINDS OF "USES"

We begin by observing that there is a variety of ways the New Testament authors can refer to the Old Testament. They can quote it directly (as Matt. 1:23 cites Isa. 7:14); they can allude to it (as John 1:1–5 alludes to Genesis 1); they can use Old Testament vocabulary with a meaning conditioned by Old Testament usage (e.g., "the righteousness of God"); they can refer to the Old Testament's broad concepts (such as monotheism and creation); and they can refer to the basic overarching story of the Old Testament (e.g., Rom. 1:1–6).

The second observation is that there is no reason to expect a single, one-size-fits-all explanation that covers every instance of the New Testament using the Old Testament. For example, an author may be intending to specify the one meaning of the Old Testament text, or he may be using the Old Testament text as providing an example or pattern that illuminates something he is writing about. He may draw a moral lesson from some event (e.g., Mark 2:25–26), and he might find an analogy between his audience and the ancient people (e.g., 1 Cor. 10:6–11). He might be making a point about how the Gentile Christians inherit the privileges of Israel (1 Pet. 2:9–10), or he might be explaining why Christians need not keep some provision of the Old Testament (e.g., Mark 7:19; Eph. 2:19). Paul describes his own calling in terms that remind us of the servant of the Lord (Gal. 1:15 evoking Isa. 49:1): since Isaiah's servant is a messianic figure (as Paul knew, see Acts 13:47; Rom. 10:16; 15:21), it is best to see Paul as likening his own calling in some way to that of the servant, rather than as claiming that he was the servant.

Text Form

This part is the least controversial. As a general rule, New Testament authors cite the Old Testament in a Greek form that is basically the Septuagint that is available in printed form today (see chap. 17). There are places where the New Testament author's citation differs slightly from that of the Septuagint: either because the author has adjusted the quotation to fit the syntax of his own sentence or otherwise adapted it to his purpose, or because he has quoted the Septuagint from memory, or because the quotation represents a textual variation. There are places where the New Testament author has apparently corrected the Septuagint in order to be closer to the Hebrew: for example, "grieve" in Ephesians 4:30 is far closer to the Hebrew of Isaiah 63:10 than the Septuagint's "provoke." In John 1:14 "full of grace and truth" may be a free paraphrase of "abounding in steadfast love and faithfulness" (Ex. 34:6).

Many Hebraists view the Septuagint as a translation with some value, but with many obvious deficiencies. The truth is, the translation quality varies with the kind of material being translated (poetry is harder than narrative), the skill of the individual translator, and the purposes of the translation (e.g., it seems that the translators of Proverbs intended to adapt the Hebrew wisdom to their setting in the high Hellenistic culture of Alexandria, at the expense of faithfully conveying the meaning of the Hebrew). More to the point, it is not clear that translational infelicities cloud any particular New Testament use of the Septuagint—generally the point for which the verse is cited depends on the part where the translation is close enough to the original.

Therefore one cannot say that, in using a Greek version, the New Testament authors have in any way slighted the original intent of the Old Testament authors.

NEW TESTAMENT REFLECTION ON THE USE OF THE OLD TESTAMENT

Several New Testament texts discuss the general stance by which Christians do, and should, approach the Old Testament. The first is Romans 1:1–6, where Paul describes the "gospel of God" as "promised beforehand through his prophets in the holy Scriptures." The content that follows narrates Jesus's public entry onto his Davidic throne through his resurrection, and Paul's apostleship as the outworking of Jesus's program "to bring about the obedience of faith for the sake of his name among all the nations": Paul is explaining that the events of Jesus's victory, and the witness of the early Christians, are just what the Old Testament had foretold. This is the kind of reading the Old Testament itself invites. Later in the same letter, Paul says, "For whatever was written in former days [i.e., in the Old Testament] was written for our instruction [i.e., as Christians]" (Rom. 15:4). He then goes on (in vv. 9–13) to cite several Old Testament texts about the expectation of the coming era when the Gentiles would receive the light and join in worship with the faithful of Israel: the mixed congregations of Jewish and Gentile Christians are the fulfillment of that hope.

In 1 Corinthians 10:1, Paul alludes to Old Testament events, saying "our fathers" experienced them. The church in Corinth, however, had a considerable proportion of converted Gentiles; so this means that Paul is treating the Gentile Christians as having been "grafted in" (Rom. 11:17–24) to the olive tree (the people of God, see Jer. 11:16), and every bit as much heirs of the story as Jewish Christians are. After listing the ways that God judged the unfaithful among the ancient people (1 Cor. 10:6–10), Paul explains that "these things happened to them as an example, but they were written down for our instruction, on whom the end of the ages has come" (v. 11). God expects those who profess to be Christians to be sure their faith is real, just as he did the people in the Pentateuch.

Hebrews 11 is able to parade the Old Testament faithful before its audience (probably mostly Jewish Christians) to show them that they must persevere in faith just as the ancients did.

In Luke 24:25–27, 44–47, Jesus "interpreted to [his disciples] in all the [Old Testament] Scriptures the things concerning himself." Luke does not tell us what that Bible study actually said. Some Christian interpreters have understood this to mean that it is possible to find in every part of the Old Testament a "foreshadowing" of some aspect of the work of Jesus. However, other interpreters think it is enough to recognize both that there are specific texts that predict the messianic work, and that the entire trend of the Old Testament story was heading toward Jesus's victory after his suffering, which would usher in the era in which the Gentiles would receive God's light (Luke 24:47, "to all nations").

BASIC CATALOG OF NEW TESTAMENT USES OF THE OLD TESTAMENT

When the apostles applied the Old Testament to New Testament realities, they were following a long line of citing earlier Scripture, using a set of practices that can be found in the Old Testament itself. For example, Old Testament writers could allude to an earlier passage and elaborate on it (e.g., Psalms 8 and 104 use Genesis 1–2); or they could allude to an earlier text and give a more precise nuance to it (as Ps. 72:17 takes the more general Gen. 22:18 and ties it specifically to the house of David). They could recognize a promise (e.g., Dan. 9:2 finding in Jer. 25:12 a promise for the length of Babylonian domination). They could see patterns of God's behavior repeated (e.g., many psalms allude to Ex. 34:6–7 as God's way of dealing with his people). They could also take texts from earlier generations and apply them to new situations (e.g., Neh. 8:14–17 is often seen as an example of actualizing the laws of Lev. 23:39–42 in concert with Deut. 16:13–15; see also the well-known pairing of Jer. 22:24–27 and Hag. 2:23).

The New Testament writers exhibit these uses due to their conviction that Christians are the heirs of Israel's story; they exhibit other uses as well due to their conviction that the resurrection of Jesus had ushered in a new era, the messianic age—"the last days" foretold by the prophets. These authors saw themselves as God's authorized interpreters for this new era that God had opened in the story of his people.

The early Christian missionaries went to synagogues to prove from the Old Testament Scriptures that Jesus is the Christ (see Acts 17:1–3; 18:26–28). This implies that they relied on and used publicly accessible arguments from the text itself, rather than merely private insights—otherwise, they would have been unjust to hold anyone responsible for failing to see something that was not truly there. Luke praises the Berean Jews, who examined the Old Testament to see whether what Paul and Silas told them was so (Acts 17:11); this implies that the New Testament invites critical interaction over its appeal to the Old Testament, and is not solely dependent on the "insider's" point of view.

In classifying these uses, the basic questions are:

- What is it about the Old Testament text that enables the New Testament writer to use it the way he does?
- What is the New Testament writer's stance toward the "original meaning" of the Old Testament text?

- What rhetorical goal is the New Testament writer trying to achieve by using the Old Testament text as he does?
- In what ways does the New Testament author resemble and differ from interpretative principles found among other interpreters who come from the same period of time, particularly other Second Temple Jewish authors who were not Christians?

The categories in this catalog are intended to be broad and suggestive; there is no substitute for a case-by-case examination of the various passages.

Promise and fulfillment. In many cases the New Testament writers understood their Old Testament texts as providing a promise about where the story was headed, and identify a particular event as the fulfillment (or partial fulfillment) of a promise. For example, Matthew 12:17–21 understood the servant of the Lord in Isaiah 42:1–3 as the Messiah, with Jesus being the promised person. Likewise, in Romans 15:12 Paul sees the spread of Christian faith among the Gentiles as fulfilling the expectation of Isaiah 11:1–10.

Pattern and fulfillment. This is often called "typology," and it refers to the way patterns found in the Old Testament enable Christians to understand their own situation in, through, and under Christ. For example, the way that a lamb in the sin or guilt offering serves as an innocent substitute to work atonement explains how Jesus's sacrifice benefits believers (compare Isa. 53:7 with John 1:29).

Analogy and application. Sometimes the New Testament writers find some kind of resemblance between their situation and an earlier one, and derive principles from the Old Testament passage for addressing the new situation. The examples of Mark 2:25–26 and 1 Corinthians 10:6–10 have already been mentioned.

When an author is using an analogy, he is not offering an interpretation of the original intent of the Old Testament text; nevertheless, the analogies respect the original intent. For example, in Matthew 21:42, Jesus uses Psalm 118:22–23 (about "the stone the builders rejected") to describe the way the Jewish leaders rejected him. Though many understand this to be a messianic prediction, the main point Jesus makes is that Jewish leaders who rejected him are (by analogy) just as wrong and wretched (Matt. 21:41) as the great world powers that thought so little of Israel (Ps. 118:22–23).

Understanding the use of analogy in this way will help when encountering some New Testament texts that are more difficult. In 1 Corinthians 9:9 and 1 Timothy 5:18, Paul cites an Old Testament law (Deut. 25:4) about not muzzling an ox, and he applies it as a justification for paying those in ministry. The Old Testament text is based on a principle of caring for working animals; Paul's application seems to be based on a "how much more should we care for those who serve us with the word" kind of argument. In Galatians 4:21–31, Paul constructs an "allegory" from Hagar and Sarah in Genesis, in order to convince his readers to reject the false teachers. There is no need to think he is disclosing any kind of additional meaning in Genesis, nor is he disregarding the original intent of the Old Testament passages; he is simply likening those who follow his message to the "children of promise" (supernaturally produced like Isaac), and those who follow the false teachers to him "who was born according to the flesh" (i.e., to Ishmael).

Eschatological continuity. "Eschatology" in the Old Testament is focused on the coming era in which the Messiah will lead his people in bringing the light to the Gentiles; the New Testament position is that this era began with the resurrection and ascension of Jesus. These are separate chapters in the unfolding story of God's work in the world, but they exhibit continuity because it is the same God at work, who saves people in the same way (see Rom. 4:1–8), who grafts believing Gentiles into the olive tree of his people (Rom. 11:17), and who is restoring the image of God in them. Hence Christian believers, both Jew and Gentile, share the privilege of the mission of Israel (e.g., 1 Pet. 2:9–10, looking back to Ex. 19:5–6 and other texts). Thus, the Ten Commandments supply moral guidance to Christians (Rom. 13:8–10). The same "righteousness of God"—God's uprightness and faithfulness in keeping his promises—that the Old Testament celebrates lies behind God's sending Jesus (Rom. 1:17).

Eschatological discontinuity. This category is related to the previous one and reflects the change in redemptive era. For example, God's faithful no longer need to observe the Old Testament food laws, whose purpose was to distinguish Israel from the Gentiles (Lev. 20:24–26; cf. Acts 10:9–23). Other aspects of the Sinai covenant are likewise no longer directly applicable to God's people, such as the sacrificial system and the theocratic government centered in Jerusalem.

Development. Psalm 72:17 does not change the promise of blessing-to-the-nations of Genesis 22:18 but rather develops it by bringing the manner of fulfillment into sharper focus. In the same way, Isaiah 52:13–53:12 certainly describes the career of the Messiah in terms of rejection and humiliation followed by vindication and victory. Death is clearly not the messianic servant's end; but resurrection is not explicit there (although it now seems to be the natural inference). Thus 1 Corinthians 15:3–4 can say, "Christ died for our sins in accordance with the Scriptures" (probably echoing Isa. 53:10), and "he was raised on the third day in accordance with the Scriptures" (developing, or clarifying, Isa. 53:10). The assumption behind these examples is that the story is moving along, and God can feed new events and insights into the process (in the case of Ps. 72:17, by giving an oracle establishing the Davidic covenant; in the case of 1 Cor. 15:4, by raising Jesus from the dead).

"Fuller sense." Christians have used the Latin term *sensus plenior* ("fuller sense") for cases where the New Testament seems to find a meaning in the Old Testament that goes much farther beyond the original intent of the earlier passage than simple development. There is every reason to allow for such cases, when one considers that God is both planning events and inspiring the biblical authors as his authentic interpreters. Nevertheless it is wise to be careful; in many cases the suggestion of *sensus plenior* stems from a misapprehension of the earlier text or of the New Testament usage (see discussion of Matt. 2:15/Hos. 11:1 below). There are some instances, however, where this does in fact seem to be what the New Testament author has done. For example, in John 1:1–5, John describes "the Word" as a divine Person active in the creation; he is echoing Genesis 1:1–2:3 but seeing something there that Moses did not say. Nevertheless, this is not out of step with Genesis. One can imagine Moses saying, if he had been presented with John's Gospel, "Well, I never thought of it that way, but now that you come to say it like that, I can see where you got it, and I like it"; that is, he would not think that his original intent had been violated. It is tenuous, however, to advocate a *sensus plenior* that dispenses with original intent.

Matthew 2:15 is often taken as a case of *sensus plenior* because it says that when the holy family took shelter in Egypt (later to return to Palestine), this was to "fulfill" the words of Hosea 11:1: "Out of Egypt I called my son." Is Matthew finding a "messianic meaning" in Hosea that no one could have seen before? Probably not; it is more likely that Matthew found in Hosea a convenient summary of the exodus that contained the term "son." (Many prophets summarize the exodus as a way of reminding Israel of their obligations to the Lord: see Amos

3:1–2.) One of Matthew's themes is that Jesus showed himself the true Messiah (the Davidic representative of Israel) by embodying all that Israel was called to be, and doing so faithfully (in contrast to Israel). So Jesus's experience "fulfilled" the pattern of the exodus, which means that this is a case of pattern and fulfillment.

Deity of Christ. New Testament authors often apply Old Testament texts to Jesus that originally applied to Yahweh, the God of Israel. For example, Hebrews 1:10–12 describes Jesus by using Psalm 102:25–27, which is about God's eternity. This is not because the psalm is directly messianic but because New Testament authors accept that Jesus is Yahweh incarnate (see John 1:1–14). Thus the New Testament uses these texts consistently with their orginal intent—they describe the Lord—and recognize that their description applies to Jesus as being no less truly the Lord than is God the Father.

In all of these cases the New Testament authors view themselves as the proper heirs and faithful interpreters of the Old Testament.

Fig. 19.1 Old Testament Passages Cited in the New Testament

This chart is adapted from the lists in the standard Greek texts, NA27 and UBS4. It may appear to include considerably fewer citations than would be expected, because it focuses only on exact quotations. The New Testament is filled with allusions to the Old Testament, so the fact that, for example, there are only five places where the New Testament gives an exact quotation of a passage from Numbers should not be used as a measure of the influence Numbers had on the biblical authors. Even though exact quotations of the Old Testament may be relatively few, the influence of the Old Testament on the thinking and language of the New Testament writers is pervasive. Further, it is often a judgment call in distinguishing between a "quotation" and an "allusion," and sometimes the New Testament author uses only a phrase from the Old Testament text.

Passages marked (lxx) denote those where the Greek translation is cited, and if the versification of the Hebrew Old Testament differs from that of English translations, the abbreviation ET (for English Translation) precedes the English verse number.

Old Testament Passage	New Testament Passage(s)
Genesis	
1:27	Matt. 19:4; Mark 10:6

Old Testament Passage	New Testament Passage(s)
2:2	Heb. 4:4
2:7	1 Cor. 15:45
2:24	Matt. 19:5; Mark 10:7–8; 1 Cor. 6:16; Eph. 5:31
5:2	Matt. 19:4; Mark 10:6
12:1	Acts 7:3
12:3	Gal. 3:8; Rev. 1:7
14:17–20	Heb. 7:1
14:20	Heb. 7:4
15:5	Rom. 4:18
15:6	Rom. 4:3, 9, 22; Gal. 3:6; James 2:23
15:13–14	Acts 7:6
17:5	Rom. 4:17
18:10	Rom. 9:9
18:14	Rom. 9:9
21:10	Gal. 4:30
21:12	Rom. 9:7; Heb. 11:18
22:17	Heb. 6:14
22:18	Acts 3:25; Gal. 3:8, 16
24:7	Gal. 3:16 (?)
25:23	Rom. 9:12
26:4	Acts 3:25
28:12	John 1:51
28:14	Rev. 1:7 (?)
47:31 (LXX)	Heb. 11:21
48:4	Acts 7:5
Exodus	
1:8	Acts 7:18
2:14 (LXX)	Acts 7:27–28
2:22	Acts 7:6
3:5	Acts 7:33
3:6	Matt. 22:32; Mark 12:26; Luke 20:37; Acts 3:13; 7:32
3:7–10	Acts 7:34
9:16	Rom. 9:17
12:11	Luke 12:35

Old Testament Passage	New Testament Passage(s)
12:46	John 19:36
13:2, 12, 15	Luke 2:23
16:18	2 Cor. 8:15
19:5–6	1 Pet. 2:9
19:12	Heb. 12:20
20:11	Acts 4:24; 14:15
20:12	Matt. 15:4; Mark 7:10; Eph. 6:2
20:12–16	Matt. 19:18; Mark 10:19; Luke 18:20
20:13	Matt. 5:21; James 2:11
20:13–17	Rom. 13:9
20:14	Matt. 5:27; James 2:11
20:17	Rom. 7:7
21:17	Matt. 15:4; Mark 7:10
21:24	Matt. 5:38
22:27 (ET 28)	Acts 23:5
23:20	Matt. 11:10; Mark 1:2; Luke 7:27
24:8	Heb. 9:20
25:40	Heb. 8:5
32:1	Acts 7:40
32:6	1 Cor. 10:7
32:23	Acts 7:40
33:19	Rom. 9:15
34:34	2 Cor. 3:16
Leviticus	
11:44	1 Pet. 1:16
12:8	Luke 2:24
18:5	Rom. 10:5; Gal. 3:12
19:2	1 Pet. 1:16
19:12	Matt. 5:33
19:18	Matt. 5:43; 19:19; 22:39; Mark 12:31, 33; Luke 10:27; Rom. 12:19; 13:9; Gal. 5:14; James 2:8
20:9	Matt. 15:4; Mark 7:10
23:29	Acts 3:23
24:20	Matt. 5:38

Old Testament Passage	New Testament Passage(s)
26:12	2 Cor. 6:16
Numbers	
6:3	Luke 1:15
12:7	Heb. 3:2, 5
16:5	2 Tim. 2:19
27:17	Matt. 9:36; Mark 6:34
30:2	Matt. 5:33
Deuteronomy	
4:24	Heb. 12:29
4:35	Mark 12:32
5:16	Matt. 15:4; Mark 7:10; Eph. 6:2
5:16–20	Matt. 19:18; Mark 10:19; Luke 18:20
5:17	Matt. 5:21; James 2:11
5:17–21	Rom. 13:9
5:18	James 2:11
5:21	Rom. 7:7
6:4	Mark 12:29, 32
6:5	Matt. 22:37; Mark 12:30, 33; Luke 10:27
6:13	Matt. 4:10
6:16	Matt. 4:7; Luke 4:12
8:3	Matt. 4:4; Luke 4:4
9:3	Heb. 12:29
9:4	Rom. 10:6
9:19	Heb. 12:21
10:20	Matt. 4:10; Luke 4:8
17:7	1 Cor. 5:13
18:15	Acts 7:37
18:15–20	Acts 3:22
19:15	Matt. 18:16; 2 Cor. 13:1; 1 Tim. 5:19
21:23	Gal. 3:13
24:1	Matt. 5:31; 19:7; Mark 10:14
25:4	1 Cor. 9:9; 1 Tim. 5:18
25:5	Matt. 22:24; Mark 12:19; Luke 20:28

Old Testament Passage	New Testament Passage(s)
27:26	Gal. 3:10, 13
29:3 (ET 4)	Rom. 11:8
29:17 (ET 18)	Heb. 12:15
30:12	Rom. 10:6
30:14	Rom. 10:8
31:6	Heb. 13:5
32:4	Rev. 15:3
32:21	Rom. 10:19
32:35	Rom. 12:19; Heb. 10:30
32:36	Heb. 10:30
32:43	Rom. 15:10; Heb. 1:6 (citing LXX)
Joshua	
1:5	Heb. 13:5
22:5	Matt. 22:37; Mark 12:30, 33; Luke 10:27
1 Samuel	
12:22	Rom. 11:1–2
2 Samuel	
5:2	Matt. 2:6
7:8	2 Cor. 6:18
7:14	2 Cor. 6:18; Heb. 1:5; Rev. 21:7
22:50	Rom. 15:9
1 Kings	
19:10, 14	Rom. 11:3
19:18	Rom. 11:4
2 Kings	
1:10, 12	Luke 9:54; Rev. 20:9
19:15	Acts 4:24
1 Chronicles	
17:13	Heb. 1:5
2 Chronicles	
2:12	Acts 4:24
18:16	Matt. 9:36
Job	
5:12	1 Cor. 3:19

Old Testament Passage	New Testament Passage(s)
16:19	Matt. 21:9; Mark 11:10
41:3 (ET 11)	Rom. 11:35
Psalms	
2:1	Acts 4:25
2:7	Acts 13:33; Heb. 1:5; 5:5
2:9	Rev. 2:27; 19:15
4:5 (ET 4)	Eph. 4:26
5:10 (ET 9)	Rom. 3:13
6:4 (ET 3)	John 12:27
6:9 (ET 8)	Matt. 7:23; Luke 13:27
8:3 (ET 2)	Matt. 21:16
8:5–7 (ET 4–6)	Heb. 2:6–8
8:7 (ET 6)	1 Cor. 15:27; Eph. 1:22
10:7	Rom. 3:14
14:1–3	Rom. 3:10–12
16:8–11	Acts 2:25–28
16:10	Acts 13:35
18:50 (ET 49)	Rom. 15:9
19:5 (ET 4)	Rom. 10:18
22:2 (ET 1)	Matt. 27:46; Mark 15:34
22:14 (ET 13)	1 Pet. 5:8
22:19 (ET 18)	Matt. 27:35; Mark 15:24; Luke 23:34; John 19:24
24:1	1 Cor. 10:26
31:6 (ET 5)	Luke 23:46
32:1	Rom. 4:7
34:9 (ET 8)	1 Pet. 2:3
34:13–17 (ET 12–16)	1 Pet. 3:10–12
34:21 (ET 20)	John 19:36
35:19	John 15:25
36:2 (ET 1)	Rom. 3:18
40:7–9 (ET 6–8)	Heb. 10:5–7
40:8 (ET 7)	Heb. 10:9
41:10 (ET 9)	John 13:18
42:6, 12 (ET 5, 11)	Matt. 26:38; Mark 14:34
43:5	Mark 14:34

Old Testament Passage	New Testament Passage(s)
44:23 (ET 22)	Rom. 8:36
45:7 (ET 6)	Heb. 1:8
51:6 (ET 4)	Rom. 3:4
53:2–4 (ET 1–3)	Rom. 3:10–12
62:13 (ET 12)	Matt. 16:27; Rom. 2:6
68:19 (ET 18)	Eph. 4:8
69:10 (ET 9)	John 2:17; Rom. 15:3
69:23 (ET 22)	Rom. 11:9
69:26 (ET 25)	Acts 1:20
78:2	Matt. 13:35
78:24	John 6:31
82:6	John 10:34
86:9	Rev. 15:4
91:11	Matt. 4:6; Luke 4:10, 11
94:11	1 Cor. 3:20
94:14	Rom. 11:2
95:7–8	Heb. 3:15; 4:7
95:7–11	Heb. 3:7–11
95:11	Heb. 4:3, 5
97:7 (LXX)	Heb. 1:6
102:26–28 (ET 25–27)	Heb. 1:10–12
104:4	Heb. 1:7
104:12	Matt. 13:32; Mark 4:32; Luke 13:19
107:26	Rom. 10:7
109:8	Acts 1:20
110:1	Matt. 22:44; Mark 12:36; Luke 20:42–43; Acts 2:34–35; 1 Cor. 15:25; Heb. 1:13
110:4	Heb. 5:6; 7:17
111:2	Rev. 15:3
112:9	2 Cor. 9:9
116:10	2 Cor. 4:13
117:1	Rom. 15:11
118:6	Heb. 13:6

Old Testament Passage	New Testament Passage(s)
118:22	Matt. 21:42; Mark 12:10; Luke 20:17; 1 Pet. 2:7
118:23	Matt. 21:42; Mark 12:11
118:26	Matt. 21:9; Mark 11:9; John 12:13; Matt. 23:39; Luke 13:35; 19:38
119:32	2 Cor. 6:11
135:14	Heb. 10:30
139:14	Rev. 15:3
140:4 (ET 3)	Rom. 3:13
145:17	Rev. 15:3
146:6	Acts 4:24; 14:15
148:1	Matt. 21:9; Mark 11:10
Proverbs	
3:11	Heb. 12:5
3:34 (LXX)	James 4:6; 1 Pet. 5:5
10:12	James 5:20; 1 Pet. 4:8
11:31 (LXX)	1 Pet. 4:18
22:8 (LXX)	2 Cor. 9:7
24:12	Matt. 16:27; Rom. 2:6
25:21	Rom. 12:20
Ecclesiastes	
7:20	Rom. 3:10
Isaiah	
1:9	Rom. 9:29
5:9 (LXX)	James 5:4
6:3	Rev. 4:8
6:9 (LXX)	Matt. 13:14; Mark 4:12; Acts 28:26
6:10	John 12:40
7:14	Matt. 1:23
8:10	Matt. 1:23
8:12	1 Pet. 3:14
8:13	1 Pet. 3:15
8:14	Rom. 9:33; 1 Pet. 2:8
8:17 (LXX)	Heb. 2:13
8:18	Heb. 2:13

Old Testament Passage	New Testament Passage(s)
8:23–9:1 (ET 9:1–2)	Matt. 4:15–16
10:3	1 Pet. 2:12
10:22	Rom. 9:27
11:2	1 Pet. 4:14
11:10	Rom. 15:12
12:2	Heb. 2:13
13:10	Matt. 24:29; Mark 13:24
22:13	1 Cor. 15:32
25:8	1 Cor. 15:54; Rev. 7:17; 21:4
26:13 (LXX)	2 Tim. 2:19
26:19	Matt. 11:5; Luke 7:22
26:20 (LXX)	Heb. 10:37
27:9	Rom. 11:27
28:11	1 Cor. 14:21
28:16	Rom. 9:33; 10:11; 1 Pet. 2:6
29:10	Rom. 11:8
29:13	Matt. 15:8–9; Mark 7:6–7
29:14	1 Cor. 1:19
29:16	Rom. 9:20
29:18	Matt. 11:5; Luke 7:22
34:4	Matt. 24:29; Mark 13:25; Luke 21:26
35:4	John 12:15
35:5	Matt. 11:5; Luke 7:22
37:16	Acts 4:24
40:3	Matt. 3:3; Mark 1:3; John 1:23
40:3–5	Luke 3:4–6
40:6	1 Pet. 1:24
40:8	1 Pet. 1:25
40:13	Rom. 11:34; 1 Cor. 2:16
42:1–4	Matt. 12:18–21
42:12	1 Pet. 2:9 (?)
42:18	Matt. 11:5; Luke 7:22
43:20–21	1 Pet. 2:9 (?)
45:14	1 Cor. 14:25
45:21	Mark 12:32; Acts 15:18

Old Testament Passage	New Testament Passage(s)
45:23	Rom. 14:11
49:6	Acts 13:47
49:8	2 Cor. 6:2
49:10	Rev. 7:16
49:18	Rom. 14:11
52:4	2 Cor. 6:17
52:5	Rom. 2:24
52:7	Rom. 10:15
52:11	2 Cor. 6:17
52:15	Rom. 15:21
53:1	John 12:38; Rom. 10:16
53:4	Matt. 8:17; 1 Pet. 2:24
53:5	1 Pet. 2:24
53:6	1 Pet. 2:25
53:7–8	Acts 8:32–33
53:9	1 Pet. 2:22; Rev. 14:5
53:12	Luke 22:37; 1 Pet. 2:24
54:1	Gal. 4:27
54:13	John 6:45
55:3	Acts 13:34
55:10	2 Cor. 9:10
56:7	Matt. 21:13; Mark 11:17; Luke 19:46
59:7	Rom. 3:15–17
59:20	Rom. 11:26
61:1–2	Luke 4:18–19
62:11	Matt. 21:5
65:1	Rom. 10:20
65:2	Rom. 10:21
65:17	2 Pet. 3:13
66:1–2	Acts 7:49–50
66:14	John 16:22
66:22	2 Pet. 3:13
66:24	Mark 9:48
Jeremiah	
5:21	Mark 8:18
6:16	Matt. 11:29

Old Testament Passage	New Testament Passage(s)
7:11	Matt. 21:13; Mark 11:17; Luke 19:46
9:22–23 (ET 23–24)	1 Cor. 1:31; 2 Cor. 10:17
10:7	Rev. 15:3, 4
12:3	James 5:5
12:15	Acts 15:16
22:24	Rom. 14:11
31:15	Matt. 2:18
31:31–34	Heb. 8:8–12
31:33–34	Heb. 10:16–17
31:33	Rom. 11:26 (?)
Ezekiel	
5:11	Rom. 14:11
11:20	Rev. 21:7
37:5	Rev. 11:11
37:10	Rev. 11:11
37:27	2 Cor. 6:16
Daniel	
3:6	Matt. 13:42, 50
7:13	Matt. 24:30; 26:64; Mark 13:26; 14:62; Luke 21:27; Rev. 1:7
9:27	Matt. 24:15
11:31	Matt. 24:15; Mark 13:14
12:11	Mark 13:14
Hosea	
1:6	1 Pet. 2:10
1:9	1 Pet. 2:10
2:1	Rom. 9:26–27
2:25 (ET 23)	Rom. 9:25; 1 Pet. 2:10
6:6	Matt. 9:13; 12:7
10:8	Luke 23:30; Rev. 6:16
11:1	Matt. 2:15
13:14	1 Cor. 15:55
Joel	
3:1–5 (ET 2:28–32)	Acts 2:17–21

Old Testament Passage	New Testament Passage(s)
3:5 (ET 2:32)	Rom. 10:13
Amos	
3:13	Rev. 4:8; 15:3
5:25–27 (LXX)	Acts 7:42
9:11	Acts 15:16
Jonah	
2:1 (ET 1:17)	Matt. 12:40
Micah	
5:1, 3 (ET 5:2, 4)	Matt. 2:6
7:6	Matt. 10:35–36; Luke 12:53
Nahum	
2:1 (ET 1:15)	Rom. 10:15
Habakkuk	
1:5	Acts 13:41
2:3	Heb. 10:37
2:4	Rom. 1:17; Gal. 3:11; Heb. 10:38

Old Testament Passage	New Testament Passage(s)
Zephaniah	
3:13	Rev. 14:5
Haggai	
2:6	Heb. 12:26
2:21	Heb. 12:26
Zechariah	
3:2	Jude 9
8:16	Eph. 4:25
9:9	Matt. 21:5; John 12:15
11:13	Matt. 27:9
12:10	John 19:37; Rev. 1:7
13:7	Matt. 26:31; Mark 14:27
Malachi	
1:2	Rom. 9:13
3:1	Matt. 11:10; Mark 1:2; Luke 7:27
3:17	1 Pet. 2:9
3:23 (ET 4:5)	Matt. 17:10; Mark 9:11

Scripture Index

203

discover more great Christian books at www.ivpbooks.com

Full details of all the books from Inter-Varsity Press – including reader reviews, author information, videos and free downloads – are available on our website at **www.ivpbooks.com**.

IVP publishes a wide range of books on various subjects including:

Biography

Christian Living

Bible Studies

Reference

Commentaries

Theology

On the website you can also sign up for regular email newsletters, tell others what you think about books you have read by posting reviews, and locate your nearest Christian bookshop using the *Find a Store* feature.

IVP publishes Christian books that are **true to the Bible** and that **communicate the gospel, develop discipleship** and **strengthen the church** for its mission in the world.